AMERICA'S HOPE

AMERICA'S HOPE

Why Every Other Civilization Has Failed and What You Can Do to Save This One

Douglas E. Brinley

DESERET BOOK

SALT LAKE CITY, UTAH

Library of Congress Cataloging-in-Publication Data

Brinley, Douglas E.
    America's hope : why every other civilization has failed and what you can do to save this one / Douglas E. Brinley.
        p.   cm.
    Includes bibliographical references and index.
    ISBN 1-59038-443-1 (alk. paper)
    1. Eschatology.   2. Book of Mormon—Prophecies—Eschatology.   3. Church of Jesus Christ of Latter-day Saints—Doctrines.   4. Mormon Church—Doctrines.
    5. United States—Forecasting.   I. Title.
    BX8643.E83B75   2005
    289.3'22—dc22   2005006510

Printed in United States of America   18961
R. R. Donnelley and Sons, Crawfordsville, IN

10   9   8   7   6   5   4   3   2   1

Contents

CONTENTS

Preface

Four civilizations have occupied the land of the American continents. The first was destroyed by flood; the second and third, by civil war. These tragic endings came after promising beginnings as righteous colonies with living prophets and a knowledge of gospel principles. The people had priesthood authority and were protected by a divine covenant with Deity whereby righteousness would secure the land to them and their posterity forever. The fourth civilization, the Gentiles, also began well when the Lord intervened to help the fledgling colonists survive British might to put in place conditions for America's birth (3 Nephi 21:4). The outcome of the Gentiles' response to the Restoration message is yet to be determined.

The Book of Mormon explains how the Jaredite civilization moved from prosperity to annihilation and how the Nephite civilization was destroyed by the Lamanites. The record of Mormon and Moroni outlines the simple covenant between God and the inhabitants: "Serve the God of the land, who is Jesus Christ" (Ether 2:12), or lose the right to live on this land. Each colony that was brought to these lands knew of Christ and His teachings, so there was little excuse for the way their civilizations ended.

Through the record of God's dealings with the Jaredites and the Lehites and Mulekites, the Book of Mormon warns the fourth group, the Gentiles, of the requirements they must meet to remain on the land. The Gentiles must learn of the covenant between God and the inhabitants of this land, for at present they are unaware that such a covenant exists. Although Deuteronomy 28–29 outlines Moses' blessings and cursings to the Israelites should they turn to wickedness in their land of promise, the Bible does not record the requirements for living on *this* promised land. Only the Latter-day Saints know of that standard for the promised land of the Americas, which is found in the Book of Mormon. The Gentiles were given this land centuries after the Lamanite disintegration (Mormon 5:15–20).

This volume outlines the elements of the covenant between God and the inhabitants of the Americas as well as the stages of decline that the former civilizations passed through as they continued to choose evil rather than good until, finally, their fate was sealed. The inhabitants of the former civilizations failed to repent after repeated efforts by prophets to call them to repentance. They "ripened in iniquity" (Ether 2:9) until they cast out the righteous from among them, which left them vulnerable to divine judgments (Alma 10:22, 23; Helaman 13:14; Ether 2:8–11). The fall of these earlier civilizations was caused by broken covenants, a lesson that must not be lost on Latter-day Saints.

Acknowledgments

I express personal thanks to Walter D. "Walt" Bowen, a friend and colleague at Brigham Young University, now retired, who years ago in an institute class at Utah State University first outlined what he humorously referred to as "the broom," the concept of early civilizations being swept from the land when the inhabitants became fully "ripened in iniquity" (Ether 2:9). Noah's people faced the "mop"!

I'm thankful to Todd Parker for his careful review of the manuscript and helpful suggestions. Vern Sommerfeldt and Dennis Largey were also kind enough to review the manuscript and make valuable suggestions. My sons David and Jonathan read initial drafts and gave helpful comments. David provided insights about principles of law.

My thanks goes also to Chris Schoebinger and Cory Maxwell of Deseret Book, both of whom encouraged this effort, while Suzanne Brady made it clear and sensible. As to the final product, however, I assume full responsibility.

1

9/11

On September 11, 2001, the lives of all Americans changed dramatically when Islamic militants killed thousands of people in an unprecedented and unprovoked attack on the World Trade Center towers in New York City. Two of four hijacked airplanes, loaded with jet fuel, slammed like missiles into the twin structures only minutes apart. Three thousand unsuspecting and innocent people were killed as the giant skyscrapers imploded from heat and fire as melting steel girders brought the giant structures to the ground in a matter of hours. Some people, trapped above the stories where the planes crashed into the buildings, were unable to get past stairways or elevators and were seen jumping to their deaths. A third commandeered plane crashed into the Pentagon military complex in Washington, D. C., while a fourth craft plowed into a Pennsylvania field as passengers apparently fought the hijackers before a target, presumably located in the nation's capital, could be destroyed.

This horrific attack represented a new kind of warfare for the United States. In past military campaigns, the enemy had a specific identity and geographical boundary, and armed conflicts had always been military might and strategy against a known aggressor. On this occasion, however, our homeland was attacked unexpectedly by unknown assailants. It was unclear, initially, who was responsible for the reprehensible acts. Americans recalled the sneak attack on Pearl Harbor in the 1940s, but at least at that time we knew the Japanese were the culprits.

Though atrocities had been committed by enemies of the United States on a foreign embassy in Kenya, troop facilities in Lebanon, and a naval ship anchored in a foreign port, our homeland had remained immune from foreign attack. However, this act of terrorism was in "our house," as the athletic-minded would say, a catastrophic surprise attack that caused a shutdown of the nation's airports, airlines, and air space. It curtailed travel for days because of the uncertainty of the enemy's intent or the extent of their infiltration.

The Aftermath

If any good news came out of the terrible carnage and suffering of that day, it was the way the citizens of the nation came together to mourn and grieve over the loss of innocent life. People recommitted themselves with patriotic fervor. The nation's flag flew everywhere, as a love for country—somewhat lacking in recent decades—was revived. Firefighters and police officers, formerly the targets of protester rocks and barbs, now became national heroes as they sacrificed their own lives to rescue trapped occupants. At first, there was no way to know that the towers would fall and heroic efforts were made to get the occupants out of the buildings. Citizens were glued to their television sets in stunned disbelief as news and pictures of the disaster paraded before their eyes. Sadly, when the twin giants fell, the survivors were few. It would not be hard for each person to recall where he was when he heard the news. It truly was a day of infamy.

The surprise bombings that took place decades earlier at Pearl Harbor, Hawaii, had been reported by radio transmission. But now, television cameras brought graphic scenes of the injured citizenry, mangled steel and smoke, right into the nation's homes in living color. National commentators gave hour by hour analysis of the unfolding tragic events while theorizing about its perpetrators. In subsequent days Americans felt a knot in their stomachs as they found work and normal activities difficult to negotiate. Athletic events were canceled or postponed out of respect for the dead and missing. Memorial services were hastily convened to pay homage to the fallen heroes, survivors, and those injured in the conflagration. Churches were filled with people jarred out of spiritual apathy as they sought answers from above. Funds for decimated families of innocent and fallen comrades were quickly raised as emotional appeals tugged at the heartstrings of every American listening to the tearful accounts of lost loved ones. Heartfelt compassion and human-itarian service were everywhere present as the nation picked up the pieces and tried to move forward. There was an evident spirit of love and compassion in the hearts of all countrymen.

How Could Such a Tragedy Happen on This Land?

Latter-day Saints, familiar with the Book of Mormon scenarios on this continent, asked a few rhetorical questions: How could such a thing happen in this land? Is this not the Lord's "base of opera-tions" from which the gospel is to go forth to the world? Is not His Church headquartered here? How could an individual or group suc-ceed in carrying out such a devastating attack on this land, our homeland? "Oh, no," we wondered. Had wickedness in the land grown to such an extent that the heavens were offended? (Ether 2:12). Had prophets warned us of this possibility? Was this the long-anticipated reason for decades of counsel to store water and food supplies? Was the Second Coming imminent? Had Armageddon begun or was it at our doors? Could this be the continuation of war to precede the Millennium? (D&C 87:6–7). Were the warnings of Mormon and Moroni really accurate, after all? Answers were wanted.

Other ominous events brought additional worries, including anthrax-tainted mail in post offices and Congressional buildings that caused several deaths and great frustration as efforts were made to locate those responsible for such deeds. It was suddenly obvious that America *was* vulnerable to attack by those who would do us harm. Our leniency in allowing others to come to this land and sup with us at our table, so to speak, was now being rewarded in the death of our citizens.

It soon became apparent that a terrorist organization, al-Qaida, headed by Arab terrorist Osama bin Laden, was likely responsible. The president of the United States brought together an international coalition to bring him and other al-Qaida operatives to justice. Afghanistan proved to be the location of both headquarters and camps of the terrorists. Retaliation strikes against Taliban and al-Qaida forces in that country lasted three months as United States air power and ground troops united with the other nations and Pastun tribal leaders to kill or force Taliban and al-Qaida insurgents into hiding. Much like the Gadianton secret society of old, however, this enemy proved elusive, even as we learned that the no-longer-secret combination was a relatively small but growing international conspiracy. A temporary government supported by the United States and sanctioned by the United Nations was put in place in Afghanistan. The citizens of that nation gained their first taste of democracy when elections were held in October 2004. Reportedly, 90 percent of the country's citizens registered to vote in the first-ever national election, in which Hamid Karzid, the interim governor, was elected the first president by popular vote.

Back home, a bi-partisan commission was called to investigate how the tragedy of 9/11 (a new word in our lexicon), could have occurred. Intelligence agencies searched for answers in an effort to determine liability for the failure. Governmental hearings scrutinized the intelligence gathering agencies to determine how such a catastrophe came about. Leaders from present and past administrations were brought before the commission in an effort to determine culpability and formulate a plan to reorganize the intelligence community into more cohesive agencies.

The actions (or inaction) of the FBI, CIA, and the president's administration were dissected as both political parties accused each other of negligence. The presidential campaign in the fall of 2004 was especially bitter as blame and invectives were hurled back and forth between candidates and parties. Humility and kindness, so evident in the aftermath of 9/11, disappeared as quickly as it had appeared. The Congress passed legislation in December 2004 to establish an intelligence head who would oversee and coordinate the nation's intelligence services.

Book of Mormon Foreshadowings

As Latter-day Saints reread the Book of Mormon during the 2004 Gospel Doctrine lessons, they found new meaning in the accounts of plunder and murder carried out by the Gadianton band. It was suddenly clear to them why President Ezra Taft Benson had pleaded for Church members to read the book more frequently and carefully and urged them to get this book into the hands of Americans and thoughtful people everywhere. As members pored over the writings of Nephi, Jacob, Mormon, and Moroni, it was evident that these authors had seen our day in vision and were plainly warning us "from the dust" (Ether 8:24; see also vv. 22–26; 1 Nephi 14:6–7; Mormon 5:9; 3 Nephi 30). The parallels between our day and that of the Nephites and Lamanites and the numerous Nephite Gadiantons were apparent. It seemed as if the daily headlines were taken from the ancient text. Intrigue and terrorism among the Nephites, Lamanites, and Jaredites sounded all too familiar to modern ears. We were reminded again of a major theme of the book: *righteousness preserves the inhabitants of this land.* The text cautioned us that secret combinations, much like termites, could overthrow any nation on this land whose inhabitants lost their spiritual bearings— their military and commercial prowess notwithstanding (Ether 8). It seemed as if the writers of the Book of Mormon were reaching out to us in a way we had never before realized. Their plainness and precision were chillingly prophetic as Moroni told of seeing our day in vision (Mormon 8:34–35).

President Benson had been right. There were secret combinations in the land, and we suddenly recognized why we had not known about them—*they were secret.* We gained a new respect for prophetic and seeric insight and this scriptural record that spoke to us of our own day with powerful testimonies and virtual case studies. The message took on new significance.

President Gordon B. Hinckley, in a general conference address, reminded Latter-day Saints of the parallel between current events and the intrigue of the ancient secret band:

> We of this Church know something of such groups. The Book of Mormon speaks of the Gadianton robbers, a vicious, oath-bound, and secret organization bent on evil and destruction. In their day they did all in their power, by whatever means available, to bring down the Church. . . . *We see the same thing in the present situation.* ("Times in Which We Live," 72; italics added)

Shadows from the Past

The former inhabitants of this land were slow to live the divine requirements of habitation. Most of the time, the Jaredites and the Nephites (and certainly present-day Gentiles) were convinced that large armies, weapon caches, and massive defense measures would protect them against any enemy—only to be proven wrong time and again. Trusting in the "arm of flesh" on this land does not work when leaders and people are wicked (2 Nephi 4:34). The Book of Mormon teaches that the only permanent cure—though in the end it proved impossible for the former civilizations—is to live the gospel of Jesus Christ and be faithful to His commandments (Ether 2:12). The principle seems clear enough: When the inhabitants of the land are righteous, the Lord blesses and protects them from their enemies. He will even fight their battles. When they are wicked, however, they have no promises, and unless they repent, they will be swept off the land when they become fully ripened in iniquity.

We learn of this promise from Lehi when he blessed his son, Nephi: "Inasmuch as thy seed shall *keep my commandments, they shall prosper* in the land" (1 Nephi 4:14; italics added). Much later, when the Nephites became wicked, this phrase was stated in the negative: "Inasmuch as ye will *not* keep my commandments ye shall *not* prosper in the land" (Omni 1:6; italics added).

Iraq Invaded

It seemed to the intelligence community of the United States and its allies that Saddam Hussein, Iraq's ruthless and tyrannical leader, was capable of major mischief not only in Iraq but in other areas of the Middle East and possibly the rest of the world. It was known that in the past he had used deadly chemical weapons to kill many in neighboring Iran and also a large number of Kurds in the northern part of his own country. The United Nations demanded that he destroy such weapons and insisted that outside inspectors confirm the materiel was destroyed. Though he initially allowed a team of inspectors to conduct a search, he later banned them from the country. Under American and UN threats and sanctions, he at last relented and inspectors were again admitted. Before any such weapons were found, and after Saddam ignored seventeen United Nations resolutions seeking his compliance, a determined American president and a number of allies took the offensive and invaded the Muslim nation. Coalition forces forced Saddam out of power, and his two sons, considered by many to be more brutal than their father, were killed in a house fight. The dictator himself was later found holed up near a farmhouse north of Baghdad and was turned over to the Iraqi legal system for judgment and punishment.

About the time Iraq was under siege, in a further threat to international peace, North Korea boasted publicly of a nuclear arsenal. It was a time of unrest for the United States and uneasiness in the world as nations once again marshaled for war. Citizens were cautioned by federal authorities to gather food, water, duct tape and plastic sheeting should terrorists use biological contaminants or nuclear materials on a community. Many Latter-day Saints likely thought immediately of the years of counsel to store food and water. When no weapons of mass destruction were found by American search teams in Iraq, politicians at home renewed the debate concerning the merits of the nation's involvement in the conflict. That dialogue, often quite vitriolic, continues to the present day. Elections in Iraq in January 2005 stunned the international community, as many braved threats from insurgents to cast their vote for a democratic form of government in this Muslim nation. How the Iraq situation plays out with a new form of government will be of keen interest in the coming years.

Our Level of Righteousness Is Key

From the Book of Mormon record it is clear that the United States' vulnerability to attack by an enemy is tied to the level of righteousness of its inhabitants. President Spencer W. Kimball explained that "if we are righteous the Lord will either not suffer our enemies to come upon us—and this is the special promise to the inhabitants of the land of the Americas (see 2 Ne. 1:7)—or he will fight our battles for us (Exod. 14:14; D&C 98:97, to name only two references of many)" ("False Gods We Worship," 6). That a foreign enemy had killed some three thousand noncombatants in the 9/11 attacks was a reminder to Latter-day Saints to check their "righteousness meter." Mormon and Moroni made it clear that the inhabitants of this land must be obedient to the principles of the gospel of Jesus Christ if they expect heavenly warnings and protection.

The Jaredite-Nephite record is clear concerning the consequences of rejecting God and His prophets, of breaking covenants, and of disregarding God-ordained laws established for the residents of this land. Latter-day Saints know what happens when the inhabitants of this land turn from righteousness to spiritually destructive behavior after once knowing the gospel of Jesus Christ. When the wicked on this land overpower the righteous, a return to God and obedience to His laws are the only insurance to bring a reversal. Though these ancient civilizations had days of renewal and recommitment to principles of righteousness, in the end all three former groups threw off their spiritual yoke and turned to practices that led to their downfall and destruction.

Ripening in Iniquity

As earlier inhabitants became "ripe in iniquity" they lost the right to live on this chosen land (1 Nephi 17:35; 2 Nephi 28:16; Alma

10:19; 37:28; Helaman 5:2; 6:40; 11:37). The terms *ripe, ripen,* or *ripening in iniquity,* so frequently used by Book of Mormon authors, describes a civilization's movement from righteousness to wickedness over time. Unlike a cycle that moves in a circular direction until it returns to its starting point (such as a clock), or a pendulum that swings first to one side and then the other, "ripening" is unidirectional. Bananas and tomatoes exhibit this characteristic. Bananas pass through various color stages of green to yellow to dark and finally to dark black. They do not then return to a green state. Tomatoes change from green to a lighter shade of green to a dull red before brightening into a deep color. Further darkening can lead to rottenness, when they are good for nothing except to be tossed out. Is there anything more unappetizing than spoiled bananas or rotten tomatoes?

In a similar way, all of the former civilizations passed through initial stages of innocence and righteousness on their way to becoming a spiritually mature civilization under divine direction. The people of each group understood gospel principles and the covenants associated with living on this land (2 Nephi 1:10; Alma 9:20–23; Ether 2:7–11). They knew of the decree to serve "the God of the land, who is Jesus Christ" (Ether 2:12). Unfortunately, the ripening process continued among these peoples until they were swept off the land by flood, civil war, pestilence, famine, earthquake, lightning, or other violent means. Interestingly, the Lord took credit for their destruction! (Mormon 8:8; 3 Nephi 9:3–12; notice the "I haves"). Though prophets repeatedly counseled the people to repent, the inhabitants continued in their destructive course until they were swept from the land by the divine broom.

Reading the Book of Mormon in our day causes us to immediately compare the spiritual condition of this nation with that of the former inhabitants. We compare the situation of the Gentiles as well as of the Latter-day Saints. President Gordon B. Hinckley expressed his concerns:

As I look to the future, I see little to feel enthusiastic about concerning the family in America and across the world. Drugs and alcohol are taking a terrible toll, which is not likely to decrease. Harsh language, one to another, indifference to the needs of one another—all seem to be increasing. There is so much of child abuse. There is so much of spouse abuse. There is growing abuse of the elderly. All of this will happen and get worse unless there is an underlying acknowledgment, yes, a strong and fervent conviction, concerning the fact that the family is an instrument of the Almighty. It is His creation. It is also the basic unit of society.

I lift a warning voice to our people. We have moved too far toward the mainstream of society in this matter. Now, of course there are good families. There are good families everywhere. But there are too many who are in trouble. This is a malady with a cure. The prescription is simple and wonderfully effective. It is love. It is plain, simple, everyday love and respect. It is a tender plant that needs nurturing. But it is worth all of the effort we can put into it." ("Look to the Future," 69; italics added)

A Message for Our Day

The message of the ancient prophets rings clearly in our ears. First, we must stop the ripening process. The Lord brought the Gentiles to this land to prepare them for the Restoration. Soon after the Constitution was ratified, a young man, Joseph Smith, was born and raised up to bring the true religion back to the earth, thereby blessing the remnants of the house of Israel (1 Nephi 15:13–14; 2 Nephi 10:7–9, 18–19). America has since become a strong, stable nation. The Constitution has worked well so far because the writers assumed that the citizens of this nation would be a God-fearing and righteous people. The free enterprise system, governmental processes, productivity, and advancements in science, research, literature, education, and technology in this land are unique in the history of the world as the Constitution protects the crucible in which resources are allocated by the invisible hand of providence. We have become a prosperous nation through the pioneers of industry and the efforts of those who founded the political system of this country. God has blessed this land with an abundance of goods and services unknown in the world's history. But now, as we approach two and a half centuries as a nation, a careful look at Gentile underpinnings reveals that the ripening process is underway. The laws of the land are being undermined, and evil and wickedness are being justified by legal edict. Amulek was speaking not just of his day but of our own day, and we are witnesses to it: "I say unto you, that the foundation of the destruction of this people is beginning to be laid by the unrighteousness of your lawyers and your judges" (Alma 10:27). When lawyers and judges find justification or loopholes to make or sustain immoral behavior that is contrary to that expected of a God-fearing population, it is apparent that the ripening process is in full swing.

What about the Present Inhabitants?

It is natural to ask, Will the ripening process continue until we suffer the same fate the former inhabitants suffered? Though the timing may be open to interpretation, shadows from the past are eerily creeping across the landscape. We can be certain of one thing: Mormon and Moroni would not have spent time writing the details of the rise and fall of the Jaredites and their own people *had such a warning to us not been necessary.* We know that the Lord would not have gone to such a great effort to preserve and restore this sacred record of earlier civilizations for our benefit had the outcome of the present civilization not paralleled closely theirs. The Book of Mormon not only helps us see what our civilization needs to do to survive temporally but shows us what we must do to be saved spiritually, as it restores doctrines lost in the apostasy following the apostolic dispensation.

The progress from righteousness to wickedness of each former civilization is chronicled here in an attempt to view more clearly how a nation like the United States *could* end up in utter destruction if divine warnings go unheeded. The ripening process, we learn from the Book of Mormon, moves inexorably forward if repentance and a return to God and His commandments are not forthcoming. Hopefully, Americans, Latter-day Saints, and members of the world community who receive the Book of Mormon will learn from the fate of these earlier civilizations and realize that they cannot remain in a state of wickedness without offending God. Righteousness of the inhabitants as they follow their prophets has always been, and will yet be, the key to survival.

2

America, the
Promised Land

The Americas—north and south—have been promised lands since creation's dawn.[1] God has preserved these continents as a haven for the righteous (Ether 13:2). Latter-day scriptures have much to say about the past, present, and future of this geographical area, more particularly the area that is now the United States of America. This nation, specifically, occupies a land of destiny, a land that has been reserved and preserved by the Lord as a "base of operations" from which the gospel would be carried worldwide in this final dispensation. Nevertheless, if the inhabitants of this land become careless, forget or ignore God, His laws, and His servants, and allow wickedness to gain a foothold to the extent that evil prevails, the land then loses its divine protection and instead becomes a land of war and calamity.

The Americas have been home to at least four different civilizations:

1. Antediluvians—those who lived on the land before the flood of Noah's day. This civilization began with Adam and Eve and continued with their posterity, including Enoch and his city, down to

the time when all but eight souls were swept from the earth in a great deluge.

2. Jaredites—a colony that came to this land in eight barges soon after the Tower of Babel incident in biblical times, possibly 2200 to 2100 B.C.[2] "Jared came forth with his brother and their families, with some others and their families, from the great tower, at the time the Lord confounded the language of the people" (Ether 1:33). This colony was given the following promise: "There shall be none greater than the nation which I will raise up unto me of thy seed, upon all the face of the earth" (Ether 1:43). How sad that this civilization, which began with such a great promise, was destroyed when the people were fully ripe in iniquity. Only two survivors—Coriantumr, the king of the Jaredites, and Ether, the prophet of the Lord— survived the great desolating civil war. Coriantumr lived long enough to be found by the people of Mulek, and he dwelt among them until his death (Omni 1:21–22). The Jaredites may have remained on the land as late as 300 B.C.

3. Lehites and Mulekites—two groups from the Jerusalem area came to the Americas around 588 B.C. Though contemporaries, they came in different migrations. In time the Nephites discovered the people of Zarahemla, or Mulekites, and the two united about 300 B.C. during the reign of King Mosiah (Omni 1:14–19). The Nephite nation eventually ripened in iniquity, and those who would not deny Jesus Christ or His gospel were eventually annihilated by the Lamanites, who remain scattered throughout the land of the Americas.

4. Gentiles—latter-day people who came to this land in the fifteenth century. Columbus was the first of the Gentiles to reach the promised land (1 Nephi 12:12). After 1492, other Gentiles came to what would later be called America. The Gentiles are the present occupants of the land. Latter-day Saints, despite being a portion of the house of Israel, are also a portion of the Gentiles (D&C 109:60).

As members of the Church, identified as Israel by patriarchal blessings, who live among the Gentiles, we have a responsibility to know and understand the answers to the following basic questions:

What happened to the earlier inhabitants of this land that caused their demise?

What must the present occupants know about the covenants and requirements of righteousness demanded by Deity of those who live on this land if they are to remain a free and prosperous people?

Is it really possible that America, despite its educational progress, technological developments, and free enterprise system, could experience the same fate as the earlier inhabitants?

Why were the Lamanites spared annihilation?

What role do Latter-day Saints play in preserving the land and preventing a repetition of the events that led to the destruction of former civilizations?

Why has America been singled out as a special place for God to initiate "a great and marvelous work" in the last days? (1 Nephi 14:7; D&C 11:1; 12:1; 14:1).

The earlier civilizations were destroyed when they ripened in iniquity. The Antediluvians, Jaredites, and Nephites are long gone. There are no identifiable descendants of these people today except for the Lamanites, who, along with Jews and Gentiles, now reside upon the land.[3] Thus, the title page of the Book of Mormon indicates that the book was "written to the Lamanites . . . and also to Jew and Gentile."

A Promised Land

What is a promised land? It is a place of "refuge, a place of safety for the saints of the Most High God" (D&C 45:66). It is a place where righteous individuals gather not only to avoid the calamities that come to the wicked but to worship and wholly serve the Lord with all their heart and mind. It is a land with a political system that allows individuals to create stable families, to build a community of decent, hard working, God-fearing people who "teach one another words of wisdom; [who] seek . . . out of the best books words of wisdom; [and who] seek learning, even by study and also by faith." These are people who "organize [themselves and] prepare every needful thing; and establish a house, even a house of prayer, a house of fasting, a house of faith, a house of learning, a house of glory, a house of order, a house of God" (D&C 88:118–19). Such individuals are anxiously seeking "immortality and eternal life" through the Father's plan of salvation (Moses 1:39). Such a people are engaged in building the kingdom of God on earth, spreading the knowledge and blessings of the gospel and priesthood to those unaware of the latter-day Restoration, a people grateful for the opportunity to exercise moral agency in an environment of political stability. Such is the plan of God, who told Enoch: "Unto thy brethren have I said, and also given commandment, that they should love one another, and that they should choose me, their Father" (Moses 7:33). In the history of the world, only a few of the Father's family have chosen the good things of life and eschewed evil.

America, a Place of Zion

The scriptures speak of a latter-day Zion to be "built upon the American continent" (Articles of Faith 10; Ether 13:3, 6), a place where "there shall be gathered unto it out of every nation under heaven; and it shall be the only people that shall not be at war one with another. . . . And it shall come to pass that the righteous shall be gathered out from among all nations, and shall come to Zion, singing with songs of everlasting joy" (D&C 45:69, 71).

The birth of this latter-day Zion began with the restoration of the gospel and the priesthood to Joseph Smith and his associates in the nineteenth century. It came after a long period of spiritual drifting and apostasy that followed the Savior's ministry, a time when external influences and the philosophies of men combined with internal pressures of church councils to influence men to change divine principles, doctrines, ordinances, and covenants to coincide with the philosophies of men. The valiant efforts of the apostles to take the message of Christianity to the world were polluted by the ideas of men, primarily of Greek and Roman origin. The early disciples of the Lord made valiant efforts to establish branches of the Church of Jesus Christ among the earth's inhabitants; however, governments at the time were tyrannical, and wicked kings sat upon thrones stained with the blood of martyrs. Sadly, by the end of the first century in the very land where Jesus was born and ministered in mortality, much of the truth that He had taught was lost or severely distorted after His death and that of His apostles.

While an apostasy was going on in that part of the world, a great civilization was flourishing across the ocean in the Americas, the new "promised land." Unfortunately, this civilization, like its counterpart in the Middle East, eventually ended in apostasy among the Nephites and tribal wars that took place among the surviving Lamanites (Mormon 8:8). The Lord kept hid from other nations the land of America until it was time to restore His gospel and priesthood in the last days (2 Nephi 1:8). This land was reserved for a work that would stretch across the width and breadth of the earth before the second coming of the Lord Jesus Christ. God raised up men in this latter-day civilization to organize a unique form of government under which people would be free to exercise moral agency and worship God without government interference. Soon after the miracle of independence and the birth of a new nation, the calling of a prophet and the restoration of the gospel and priesthood commenced, allowing the organization of the Lord's true Church in 1830.

On this land of promise, the Lord established the latter-day nation and then the kingdom of God which Daniel had foreseen (Daniel 2:44). Settling this new land was difficult for the initial settlers. The Pilgrims, Puritans, and others suffered extreme exposure and hardship, and many died trying to establish a foothold on the land. After a tremendous effort, and no doubt aided by divine intervention, they did it—they survived and, in time, prospered. They forged a new nation with a form of government that gave dignity to man in an environment of religious and political freedom.

The Final Dispensation

At this time in our nation's history, however, we are beginning to see ominous signs of the very things that destroyed earlier civilizations. Iniquity is becoming more rampant and acceptable despite the seeming blessings of a "soft life" God has given us. Consider the labor-saving devices and marvelous medical and technological breakthroughs of the past two centuries. It is a time of contrast, for the close of the twentieth century, perhaps the bloodiest period of war and devastation in the history of the world, was also a time when civilization moved ahead by leaps and bounds. Two world wars and several deadly skirmishes combined with an unprecedented disregard for human life by leaders in Germany, Russia, and elsewhere who killed millions of innocent people. Of course, modern warfare can kill many more people than was possible in the days of swords, knives, and other primitive weapons.

Our land has been blessed with remarkable advances in science, technology, medicine, education, entertainment, and we are witnesses to a multitude of daily world events through the miracle of satellite, television, and the Internet. Personal travel to various destinations on the planet has increased as travel time has been reduced to hours rather than days or months. The sad counterpoint to this good news is the Lord's statement to Joseph Smith in 1837 that "darkness covereth the earth, and gross darkness the minds of the people, and all flesh has become corrupt before my face" (D&C 112:23). Wickedness, the Savior told his disciples, would become so prevalent in the latter days that it would rival "the days of Noah" (Joseph Smith–Matthew 1:41), when "every man" was "evil continually" (Moses 8:22).

Yet we also find a promise in the Book of Mormon that "a New Jerusalem should be built upon this land" (Ether 13:6), and that Enoch and his city will return with the Savior to join the righteous inhabitants of the latter-day Zion (Moses 7:62–64). So, an interesting future lies ahead of us. The Lord restored His Church as a part of the preparatory work that will culminate in His return to usher in the Millennium. Latter-day Saints, despite what some may see as dismal prospects, have reason to rejoice in the promises made to the righteous.

America as a Land of Restoration

The Restoration, as Latter-day Saints refer to it, came after a long night of apostasy. And despite attempts at reform by good and sincere men in Great Britain and Europe, it was here, in America, that the Lord restored His Church and priesthood. This is the land where He sent heavenly messengers to return the fulness of the gospel and restore divine authority to administer essential priesthood ordinances and establish His Church. It was on this soil that He inspired men to form a new nation. It was on this territory that mankind could once again exercise agency with minimal government interference in a representative form of political system rare in the earth's history.

Soon after the founding of this nation, God the Father and His Son Jesus Christ chose to reveal themselves to a young, unsophisticated, and unlettered fourteen-year-old boy, who would declare the principles of salvation and exaltation that had been missing from the earth for most of two millennia. Moroni revealed to Joseph Smith the location of gold plates that contained the writings of prophets who lived anciently on these continents and made an account of the Lord's dealings with their people. Mormon, after whom the book is named, abridged centuries of record keeping on a set of metal plates of his own making. At his death, the records passed to Moroni, his faithful son who witnessed the divine broom sweep from the earth the last of the Nephites who would not deny the gospel and unite with the Lamanites. Before their deaths, both Mormon and Moroni were shown our day by the Lord (3 Nephi 30; Mormon 8:34–40), and the two warned us against committing the same follies that destroyed their people and the earlier Jaredite civilization. They outlined the principles of life and death for us, assuring us that if we did as earlier groups had done, we too would suffer the same fate.

Latter-day Scope

The work of God on the earth began in this land of promise with our first parents, Adam and Eve.[4] Now, in these last days, the gospel is being spread worldwide from this sacred soil. President Ezra Taft Benson was fond of saying that "America, the land of liberty, is the Lord's latter-day base of operations for His restored church" ("Our Divine Constitution," 4). It is from this land of free enterprise and religious freedom that most of the Church's missionaries have embarked to scour the globe in search of Israel's remnants.

In vision, Nephi saw Christopher Columbus, a latter-day Gentile, discover this land centuries after the destruction of Nephi's people and the decline of the Lamanites. Nephi then saw that other Gentiles would stream to these shores (1 Nephi 13:14–15). The Savior previewed the work that would be done among the Gentiles in the last days. "It is wisdom in the Father," He taught the Nephites, "that they [the Gentiles] should be established in this land, and be set up as a free people by the power of the Father, that these things [the Book of Mormon] might come forth from them unto a remnant of your seed, that the covenant of the Father may be fulfilled which he hath covenanted with his people, O house of Israel" (3 Nephi 21:4). So, America's latter-day destiny was known in former days.

The Book of Mormon is a general handbook of instructions that outlines the requirements for the inhabitants of the land. Latter-day prophets, like those of an earlier time, again lift the warning voice to urge us to avoid the wickedness and depravity that seem to slip into a society when people become careless in their treatment of sacred things. The counsel of modern prophets, seers, and revelators comes as a warning to us to avoid the stages through which the earlier civilizations passed.

Ascent and Decline

It was not by accident that these original colonies came to these shores. They came under divine direction. And for a brief time each group seemed determined to live righteously (Laman and Lemuel were notable exceptions). The decline and destruction of every civilization can now be viewed with some objectivity as the events that took place came in inexorable stages. In hindsight we can see that the fall of these earlier nations was not a mysterious process. The sequence is not difficult to trace because the Book of Mormon clearly spells out the general scenario: the Lord leads a group of righteous people to this land where they covenant to serve Him and obey His commandments. However, if they rebel against Him to the extent that they break their covenant and reach a level of wickedness set by the Heavenly Judge, they forfeit the right to live on the land. If they fail to repent and turn from their wickedness after prophets and missionaries call them to repentance, they suffer divine consequences and, unless they repent, are destroyed. The Lord does not tolerate wickedness, for as He informed Joseph Smith, "I the Lord cannot look upon sin with the least degree of allowance" (D&C 1:31).

Could the Past Be Repeated?

The question of whether the same calamities that befell the earlier inhabitants could take place again on this land is an important query. As citizens of the United States today, many may think it does not seem possible for us to suffer the same fate as the Jaredites and Nephites suffered, and certainly not the fate of the Antediluvians. Surely we are too advanced, too powerful, we tell ourselves, to suffer the fate of the earlier inhabitants. Our civilization is too diverse, too sophisticated, too complex, we argue, to have such a thing take place. These are modern times, and conditions are so different. We are not living in the time when superstition reigned among the uneducated, uncivilized, and unsophisticated. That same reasoning was espoused by the Jaredites and Nephites at various times. But the fact that the Lord preserved this record and brought it forth in our own day lends credence to the warning that such an ending is possible.

Latter-day Saints

Latter-day Saints occupy an interesting position in the last days scenario. Prominent Church members now sit in influential posts of government, business, industry, commerce, law, and education. Our missionary force stretches worldwide to proclaim the truth about Jesus Christ and His ministry and gospel. And we know from latter-day scriptures that any ideology or theology that is not Christ-centered but man-made will ultimately end in failure.

Church members have an obligation to be missionaries in carrying to others the theme of covenants and righteousness on this land. As we establish ever widening enclaves of Saints in many countries of the world, this message must be spread quickly. Surely we are now nearer the time Nephi spoke of when he said, "I, Nephi, beheld the power of the Lamb of God, that it descended upon the saints of the church of the Lamb, and upon the covenant people of the Lord, who were scattered upon all the face of the earth; and they were armed with righteousness and with the power of God in great glory" (1 Nephi 14:14).

Latter-day Saints have an interest in the spiritual progress of the Gentiles among whom we live because we are part of them. It is imperative that Church members understand the laws of spiritual survival that pertain to inhabiting this land. The Saints must be a major catalyst to influence this nation's citizens to meet more squarely its responsibilities and obligations to the God of this land. Any objective soul should recognize that, historically, the Lord has given preferential treatment to this territory on the planet. We must understand, as Church members, that we *can* affect the spiritual condition of the present inhabitants if we make the effort. It is called "missionary work." All Church members are responsible, not just those called as full-time proselyters. It is not an easy assignment the Lord has given us, however, because the wicked never like to be told they are wicked, and the inhabitants of the land have become so self-sufficient that they are even less likely to humble themselves and call upon the God of heaven to preserve them.

As Latter-day Saints, we may find that our danger is not wholesale apostasy from the truth, as happened following the Lord's ministry or on this land following the Nephite-Lamanite wars, but with the test of wealth. Israel has proven in the past how complacent people can become living in relative peace and surrounded by many blessings. We can become indistinguishable from the Gentiles. Yet we simply must not adopt the attitudes, secular thinking, and perverse immorality so prevalent in our society. Our youth must not imitate the tattooed and body-pierced among us or adopt immodest dress styles and personal behaviors repulsive to heaven. We must not be lured away from our goal to "come unto Christ" (Omni 1:26) and to take the gospel to the world, perfect the Saints, and redeem the dead.

There is always the possibility that we will fall asleep and become diverted from our mission to warn the Gentiles of the requirements of righteousness that attend this land (2 Nephi 28:21–22). With the present size of the Church, our success in missionary efforts must become more productive in the days ahead. We are to be leaders in this renewal of righteousness in the land and in the world, for who else knows that covenants exist and consequences stare us in the face should we choose wickedness and depravity over righteousness.

The Role of the Book of Mormon

The Book of Mormon gives significance to the role and mission of The Church of Jesus Christ of Latter-day Saints. As a people, we have a responsibility to get this book of scripture into the hands of the Gentiles. We make it simple for anyone to obtain a copy of the scriptures, as DVDs and "pass-along cards" spark interest in our message. We are to flood the earth with the Book of Mormon, reading it ourselves so that we might understand the spiritual requirements for an inheritance in this land. The stick of Joseph—another name for the Book of Mormon record—outlines the only way to avoid the ripening process, coming forth as it does in the very land where its warnings are most relevant, poignant, and practical.

Because of America's place as an economic and political power among the nations of the world, it is critical that Latter-day Saints understand their role in living gospel principles so that people everywhere, faced with spiraling physical and spiritual pollution, will be drawn to the Church and its teachings. Latter-day Saints must heed the call to stand as a beacon of light in a world ripening in iniquity and gross darkness. We must sustain the principles of a republic also, for if America fails, the Church will find it difficult to carry out its mandate to take the gospel and the priesthood worldwide. The Church can prosper only in an environment of political freedom and economic prosperity. It is nearly impossible to promulgate the message of Christ under conditions of political tyranny where individual agency is restricted. (Consider the difficulty of taking the gospel to the nations of modern Islam.) This nation of America cannot be the base from which to operate worldwide if our political system disregards the dignity of men, women, or children. Too, the spread of the gospel requires an economic standard of living that supports a worldwide missionary effort. So far, the productivity of our free enterprise system, despite occasional blips, has been more than equal to the task.

It is little wonder that the Restoration took place in this land which was prepared by God for an important latter-day mission. What other nation has created the economic productivity to sustain a people with the divine charge to cover the globe with its emissaries? What other country, for that matter, could have hosted the Restoration? Even when grounded in an environment of freedom and under the protective shield of the Constitution, the Lord's Church was dealt a severe blow when its first prophet was killed in a jail in Illinois on June 27, 1844. The Church was, in this supposed land of freedom, forced out of the Union into Mexican Territory.

Now in the first decade of a new millennium, the Church is growing dramatically under the direction of prophets, seers, and revelators. It will continue to do so. The Church is establishing a presence in this land and throughout the free world wherever it is legally recognized. Latter-day Saints seek to share the gospel with the rest of the Father's family in each nation where honest souls will listen to the message of salvation and accept it. As sufficient numbers of members and priesthood leaders are achieved, chapels and temples are built so that the work of God is not only established in the land but moves forward.

The Lord asks the Saints to send their young men and many of their young women and retired couples as a missionary force commissioned to bring people to Christ through the principles and ordinances of the gospel. Their good works are helping the Church to come forth even more "out of obscurity and out of darkness, the only true and living church upon the face of the whole earth" (D&C 1:30). The success of the Saints in bringing the gospel to the Gentiles is an important work from which the Saints must not shy away. So much that lies in futurity depends on our ability to influence the Gentiles to join with us in a way of life compatible with the principles of the gospel.

The Book of Mormon teaches us how to avoid the fate of the earlier inhabitants of the land. No wonder President Ezra Taft Benson made it a major theme of his ministry to prick the conscience of Latter-day Saints to read and get acquainted with the details of this record. President Gordon B. Hinckley has consistently pleaded with the Saints to sup from its pages:

> If the Book of Mormon is true, then this land is choice above all other lands; but if it is to remain such, the inhabitants of the land must worship the God of the land, the Lord Jesus Christ. The histories of two great nations, told with warning in this sacred volume, indicate that while we must have science, while we must have education, while we must have arms, we must also have righteousness if we are to merit the protection of God. (*Teachings of Gordon B. Hinckley,* 39–40)

How can the Latter-day Saints understand the coming events unless they are acquainted with the details of the sacred text? How can Latter-day Saints warn the Gentiles of their sins and errors if their own skirts are bloodstained? We cannot help the Gentiles if we ourselves don't know the rules of proprietorship. America was set up by the Lord in these last days as a model for the world to understand how personal agency operating in a free enterprise system provides both economic and political blessings. When an environment of religious freedom abounds, the work of God moves forward in the land.

The Voice of Warning

Historically, Israel has never mixed well with its Gentile neighbors. In these last days, we are living amongst them. We live side by side on the same streets. It is true that many Gentiles have fought this work of the Lord from the very beginning of this dispensation. In many ways, progress has been slow. The Church suffered severe persecution in the past. Hopefully, those days are now past as the civil rights movement in the United States has also benefited the Saints in that our missionaries are free to proselyte and they are not imprisoned or threatened with legal action for preaching the gospel in public—yet. Latter-day Saints are free to travel the streets and byways, sharing the message of the Restoration. Our task now is to attract the honest in heart to the message of the Restoration.

In 1995, for example, the First Presidency and the Quorum of Twelve Apostles issued a document entitled "The Family: A Proclamation to the World." This message to the world states the position of the Church regarding the importance of marriage and family relations in the plan of salvation. Issues of marriage and family are common themes among all people and cultures. Perhaps the principles of a stable and strong marriage and a happy family life will be a significant key by which we, as a people, attract others to the gospel, especially when more and more churches, it seems, ignore the sin of living together without marriage or capitulate to the advocates of legalizing same-gender relationships.[5]

There are numerous prophecies to the effect that if the Latter-day Saints will live the principles of the gospel at home and in the workplace, we will draw honest and decent people into the kingdom. For example, President Harold B. Lee promised:

> I say to you Latter-day Saint mothers and fathers, if you will rise to the responsibility of teaching your children in the home—priesthood quorums preparing the fathers, the Relief Society the mothers—the day will soon be dawning when the whole world will come to our doors and will say, "Show us your way that we may walk in your path" (see Micah 4:2). (*Teachings of Harold B. Lee,* 277)

President Spencer W. Kimball observed:

> Many of the social restraints which in the past have helped to reinforce and to shore up the family are dissolving and disappearing. The time will come when only those who believe deeply and actively in the family *will be able to preserve their families in the midst of the gathering evil around us.* ("Families Can Be Eternal," 4; italics added)

Elder Boyd K. Packer predicted:

> Across the world, those who now come [into the Church] by the tens of thousands will inevitably come as a flood to where the family is safe. Here they will worship the Father in the name of Christ, by the gift of the Holy Ghost, and know that the gospel is the great plan of happiness, of redemption. ("Father and the Family," 21)

Summary

Can the present inhabitants of the land live the laws of civility and sustain a Christ-friendly environment? Can this nation rise to its tallest spiritual stature under the banner of an inspired Constitution that grants among its privileges freedom of religion? Will America, with its magnificent potential to lift the dignity of men and women above the animal plane, lead the world back to a level of sanity and common sense, or is it our destiny to tread the same path as did the ancients on this land? Will the people of this nation (and ultimately the world community) choose the gospel and teachings of Jesus Christ over secular and humanistic philosophies? Is persecution of the righteous inevitable? Will good win out over evil? Will this land's citizens eventually "come unto Christ" (Moroni 10:32). Or were the warnings of Mormon and Moroni wasted on an affluent, arrogant group of ingrates who will have to face, with certainty, divine judgments because they ripened in wickedness to the point where the only recourse is destruction?

Many principles and issues are involved. If they are understood, the errors and weaknesses of former civilizations in the Americas may teach us what to avoid. We must recognize our own shortcomings and make significant changes in our behavior if we are to avoid the sweep of the divine broom.

3

America: Past, Present, and Future

The authors of the Book of Mormon foresaw that we would take the same dangerous path as their people did. They used every metal plate to plead, sermonize, and provide us with parallels and warnings from their time to awaken us to the dangers of wickedness and iniquity in our own day. They feared we might duplicate the tragic ending of their own people. In addition, Mormon and Moroni abridged records and sermons of earlier Nephites when prophetic messages fell on deaf ears. This father-son combination cried out to us to understand that those who live upon this land have no guarantee of peace and prosperity if they choose wickedness over righteousness. They waved a red flag at us to spiritually shake us, as best they could, as a voice crying from the dust (2 Nephi 33:13). They wanted us to understand that although a society can move from a righteous beginning to a larger, more stable and progressive nation, it can also, sadly, move to a state of spiritual apathy, iniquity, gross wickedness, and eventual annihilation. These authors knew that if we of the last dispensation failed in our ministry, if we were to become as wicked as were the people who lived in their day and even earlier times, not only would we be destroyed but all their efforts to warn us would be in vain. So they made a heroic effort to outline the dangers confronting us and from their experiences provided us with solutions.

We learn from their writings, for example, that Americans have inherited a unique set of promises and cautions: "This is a choice land, and whatsoever nation shall possess it shall be free from bondage, and from captivity, and from all other nations under heaven" (Ether 2:12). On the other hand, we learn that "whatsoever nation shall possess it shall serve God, or they shall be swept off when the fulness of his wrath shall come upon them" (Ether 2:9).

When we see what happened to the earlier civilizations, we realize the Lord was true to His word. Though the former inhabitants were blessed in times of righteousness, they eventually were swept to destruction in dramatic fashion. We are now beginning to show classic signs of the same disease and decay that afflicted the previous inhabitants. The former occupants also built societies and cities thought to be indestructible and invincible, only to be completely destroyed by God himself. "And behold, *it is the hand of the Lord which hath done it*" (Mormon 8:8; italics added). In the days of King Noah, the Lord promised a similar fate unless the people repented: "Except they repent and turn to the Lord their God, behold, I will deliver them into the hands of their enemies" (Mosiah 11:21).

As the present inhabitants of the Americas, we live under a similar set of rules and promises. We face the same two options they did: build a righteous society as Enoch did millennia ago and reach unprecedented heights as civilized people before the Lord comes again, or, forget God and spiritually fall on our faces as did the people of Noah, Jared, and Nephi. Both scenarios are possible, of course, but as Israelites living on the land of Joseph (3 Nephi 15:12–15) in this final dispensation, we are expected to build the New Jerusalem and are eligible to build it. Ancient prophets foresaw that such a city would be built on this land (Ether 13:3–6; Moses

7:62–63), and latter-day scriptures contain the blueprints. Great promises are extended to the righteous of our day while the threat of destruction hangs over the head of the wicked.

Long-Range Perspectives

Though there are disturbing prophecies concerning this nation, principles from the Book of Mormon and the Doctrine and Covenants explain how a civilization can rise to great spiritual heights only to fall apart when the people choose evil over good. These principles remain alive and relevant to our own spiritual survival. These principles come from the scriptural records and from those whom the Lord has called to counsel us in our day and time. Faithful Latter-day Saints are wise to follow the lead of the living prophet, the "watchman upon the tower" (D&C 101:45) who has the responsibility to warn us and caution us as individuals, families, nations, and a community of believers. Blessings and divine protection are promised the faithful. We want to avoid the certain penalties that come upon the wicked (Alma 10:23; Helaman 13:13–14).

There is still time to turn this nation back to God and a state of righteousness. The followers of Christ are always optimistic that God is in charge. It is not too late. By listening to the last decade of general conference addresses, for example, a listener would not detect panic among the Lord's servants. Warnings and pleadings to live the gospel and be faithful to our covenants abound, of course, but no prophet has yet predicted an end-of-the-world scenario or even specific judgments in the immediate period ahead, as did Samuel to the Nephites (Helaman 14:3–5, 20). What our prophets are telling us, however, is to get our houses in order—financially, spiritually, and otherwise—and to shore up our relationships as married couples and families because the mission of the Church now and in the foreseeable future will require strong and stable individuals to assist the Lord in this final dispensation. The effort needed to fulfill our responsibilities to each other and to the Gentiles in the years ahead will test the resolve of every Latter-day Saint. There will be some dark days ahead, as we have learned from 9/11 and the war in Iraq. We enjoyed a window of peace and prosperity the last three decades of the previous century. We were given an opportunity to carry out the mission of the restored gospel among our fellow citizens in times of peace. How long that window will remain open is yet unknown, but we know that the day will come when it will close (D&C 29:14–20; 34:7–9; 45:26; 87:6–7; 88:91). Perhaps the war in Iraq is the turning point in peace versus wars that culminate in the second coming of the Lord Jesus Christ.

Church leaders are uncomfortable, and justifiably so, with those who take it upon themselves to expound personal theories on exactly when major events will take place. We rely on the prophetic voice of inspiration, particularly that of the president of the Church, to inform us of how God expects us to respond to the events ahead. His counsel will be even more important in the coming years: "Wherefore, meaning the church, thou shalt give heed unto *all his words and commandments* which he shall give unto you as he receiveth them, walking in all holiness before me. For his word ye shall receive, as if from mine own mouth, in all patience and faith. For by doing these things *the gates of hell shall not prevail against you*" (D&C 21:4–6; italics added). There is safety in following the Brethren. As we will see with the Jaredite civilization, failing to follow the counsel of a living prophet cost those inhabitants their lives. We don't need to know the day and the hour when judgments will come upon the earth, and for good reason. Elder Gordon B. Hinckley said many years ago: "To know when they [the fulfillment of prophecies and judgments] will come would take from us much of the self-discipline needed to walk daily in obedience to the principles of the gospel" ("We Need Not Fear His Coming," 83).

On the other hand, there is no excuse for any Latter-day Saint to be unfamiliar with scriptures that outline, in general terms, what lies ahead. The record of Mormon was written especially for us, and the Doctrine and Covenants is a handbook on how to bring to pass an Enoch-like Zion in this last dispensation. As Church members we must not be ignorant of the signs of the times for that was a major contribution of biblical seers and Book of Mormon prophets who clearly saw the events of our day. If we are familiar with past and future events, we have a longer-range perspective to understand the relevance of the warnings of our leaders.

The Lord's pattern of having His servants teach the people what they must know is always an early warning system, never alarmist or last minute. Even though scriptures can be graphic about coming events, His prophets, seers, and revelators illuminate the sequences so that when we are witnesses to such events, we realize that we were given sufficient time to prepare.

Who can doubt, however, that we *are* moving into an exciting period of the earth's history? The Church's name, given by revelation, identifies us as living in the latter times, a period of great turmoil (D&C 115:4–6). We read that "after the opening of the seventh seal, before the coming of Christ," important events will take place that will test the faith of the righteous and bring judgments and destruction to the wicked (D&C 77:13). Latter-day scriptures indicate cataclysmic events ahead (2 Nephi 27:1–3; 28:32; 3 Nephi 16:10:14–15, 21; D&C 29:14–21; 84:96–97; 87:5–7; 88:84–85, 87–91). Our task, as disciples of Jesus Christ living in these days of prophecy, is not to panic but to work our own stewardships. We monitor personal responsibilities of self, family, church, and neighbors—managing well that which is within our stewardship and power. As we do so, we also keep our eyes and ears attuned to the Lord's prophets and the events of the day. If we live our lives in harmony with current and future revelation, are faithful to our covenants with the Almighty, sustain Church leaders, and monitor governmental processes through an awareness of current events and use of the ballot box, then promises of protection exist (D&C 98:10). Covenants are our primary source of spiritual protection.

So, while prophecy may cause genuine trepidation, the prophets of our day remain optimistic and upbeat about the immediate future. The Church is moving ahead under their direction, and we have only scratched the surface in response to the Lord's command to take the gospel to every nation, kindred, tongue, and people. Prophets know too that prophecy may be conditional—that the righteousness of the people can delay or suspend divine judgments. So if our leaders are optimistic, we should be, too. They are telling us not to fold up the tent just yet. They are asking us not to get caught up in trying to time the statements of dead prophets when they, as living prophets, are giving us our marching orders to move ahead.

Many events that must take place before the second coming of the Lord will test the faith of the Saints. But there are also promises to the righteous, as Nephi reminded us: "Wherefore, he will preserve the righteous by his power, even if it so be that the fulness of his wrath must come, and the righteous be preserved, even unto the destruction of their enemies by fire. Wherefore, the righteous need not fear; for thus saith the prophet, they shall be saved, even if it so be as by fire" (1 Nephi 22:17).

This is the Lord's Church. He is in charge and knows what He is doing. He instructs His prophets as He has done from the beginning. Missionaries have been sent forth to teach and warn His other children, and He will preserve both the Church and the Saints if they are faithful to their covenants. The Church will not be destroyed. That is sure and positive! (See chapter 14.)

Individuals may stumble. Some may lose heart and faint in the trenches, and some may even surrender to the opposing forces, but the faithful will go on about their Father's business. When every member lives the gospel and models righteousness, is willing to share divinely revealed truths with those unacquainted with them, then the hearts of men and women can change and the nation can likewise make dramatic changes. When individuals understand the plan of salvation and their relationship to Deity, when they comprehend the purposes of mortality, and eternity, and the mission of Jesus Christ, then they will, of their own agency and in sufficient numbers, change their behavior to conform to the principles of the plan of salvation. Elder Neal A. Maxwell explained how understanding the plan of salvation is an important key to our happiness as a people:

> One of the great blessings flowing from amplifying, latter-day revelations is the crucial, doctrinal framework known as the marvelous plan of salvation, the plan of happiness, or the plan of mercy. . . .
>
> So vital is this framework that if one stays or strays outside it, he risks provinciality and misery. In fact, most human misery represents ignorance of or noncompliance with the plan. A cessation of such mortal suffering will not come without compliance to it. ("Great Plan of the Eternal God," 21)

The Future of the Gentiles

We live in the times of the Gentiles (Joseph Smith-History 1:41; D&C 45:25, 28, 30). Gentiles, from the Book of Mormon perspective, are latter-day Christians who presently reside and govern the land. They have been blessed with unprecedented political freedom, prosperity, leisure time, and a plethora of goods and services from which we may choose. As Latter-day Saints living in their midst, we have been blessed by their ingenuity. Nonetheless, the Gentiles are mired in a state of apostasy. They are unaware that the Lord has spoken again in our day and age. We must get their spiritual attention through our good works and messages, hoping that it will cause them to look seriously at the work of God that is progressing throughout the earth (D&C 86:11). We need to acquaint them with the Book of Mormon and the additional revelations and principles of the restored gospel to add to their foundational belief in Jesus Christ. If we will do our part and they theirs, dramatic changes can take place. Even people outside the Church have predicted that our growth rate, if continued, will make us a major religious force in the world.[1]

Summary

Book of Mormon prophets saw our day and reached out over the expanse of time to assist us. We can profit from their counsel and reap the blessings that are available to us, or we can ignore them, rebel against the work of God in this latter day, join in the immorality of the Gentiles, and be destroyed just as were the former inhabitants. The message of the ancient prophets is clear: *America is consecrated as a promised land forever if its inhabitants are willing to serve the God of the land, who is Jesus Christ.*

As we study carefully the civilizations on this land before the Gentiles came, we have a benchmark to help us evaluate the spirituality and progress of the current inhabitants. We can observe trends and assess the spiritual component of the Gentiles to see if we are headed for a destructive cycle or if this time we build Zion and gather the righteous together (D&C 45:65–71). The Lord has provided sufficient revelation and knowledge for us to succeed with our Gentile neighbors if we will open our mouths (D&C 60:2).

The prophets of past dispensations anticipated our times with excitement and awe. The Lord told the Prophet Joseph Smith while he and others languished in Liberty Jail:

God shall give unto you knowledge by his Holy Spirit, yea, by the unspeakable gift of the Holy Ghost, that has not been revealed since the world was until now;

Which our forefathers have awaited with anxious expectation to be revealed in the last times, which their minds were pointed to by the angels. (D&C 121:26–27; italics added)

The prophets from Adam down to Jesus Christ and the righteous on this continent anciently looked forward to a latter-day period of revelation and restoration, a fulfillment of blessings reserved for a future time. How fortunate we are to be the ones who live in the days foreseen by the prophets of old! How blessed are we who live upon this promised land with such a comfortable standard of living. It is a wonderful time to be on the earth, even when the winding-up scenes are taking place right before our eyes, some of them quite sad and disconcerting. It is a time of contrasting evil and righteousness, a time when the blessings of the Lord are being showered upon those who live the gospel but also a time when wickedness is reaching levels that undermine the work of God. We are gaining sufficient numbers of committed members of the Church to carry the message of the Restoration to a worldwide audience as God opens the doors for the spread of the gospel in these latter days.

When, for example, in the history of this planet, have the disciples of Jesus Christ numbered in the millions? And yet we are humbled by the fact that the world is ripening in wickedness to such an extent that, in many ways, we are approaching the filth of Noah's day (Moses 8:22; Joseph Smith–Matthew 1:41–42). Surely the Lord has great expectations for the Latter-day Saints.

4

Those Who Warned Us

The four principal authors of the Book of Mormon were impressive record keepers. Mormon, after whom the book is named, is responsible for 63 percent of the text. His son Moroni, who was one of the last surviving Nephites,[1] accounted for 10 percent of the record. Nephi began recording his account after arriving in the promised land and is responsible for 22 percent of the present volume. Jacob, his younger brother, contributed 4 percent to the volume. Other authors at the end of the small plates of Nephi include Enos, Jarom, Omni, Amaron, Chemish, Abinadom, and Amaleki, who was born during the reign of Mosiah, the father of King Benjamin. Amaleki wrote about his own day, and he lived to witness King Benjamin bring peace to the war-torn land. Before his death, Amaleki explained why he delivered the small set of gold plates to the king: "Having no seed, and knowing king Benjamin to be a just man before the Lord, wherefore, I shall deliver up these plates unto him" (Omni 1:25). The two records of Nephi, the small and large plates, were now together in the possession of the righteous monarch.

Each Author Receives a Visitation from the Savior

Each of the four major authors of the Book of Mormon had a visitation from Jesus Christ. Mormon wrote of his experience, "And I, being fifteen years of age and being somewhat of a sober mind, therefore *I was visited of the Lord, and tasted and knew of the goodness of Jesus*" (Mormon 1:15; italics added). The Lord apparently added an assignment to that given him by Ammaron to "engrave on the [large] plates of Nephi all the things that ye have observed concerning this people" in the fourteen-year period to follow (Mormon 1:4). The young prophet ended up abridging a millennium of earlier writings from Lehi down to his own day of calamity.

Mormon's son, Moroni, referred to his experience with the Savior. In a farewell to the Gentiles, he said that at the Judgment "shall ye know that I have seen Jesus, and that *he hath talked with me face to face, and that he told me in plain humility, even as a man telleth another in mine own language,* concerning these things" (Ether 12:39; italics added).

Nephi strongly desired to "know of the mysteries of God," and in his quest to learn the will of the Lord, he said: "I, Nephi, being exceedingly young, . . . and also having great desires to know of the mysteries of God, wherefore I did cry unto the Lord; and behold *he did visit me,* and did soften my heart that I did believe all the words which had been spoken by my father" (1 Nephi 2:16; italics added). Nephi also recorded that heavenly messengers visited him (2 Nephi 4:24–25), and he acknowledged that both he and his younger brother Jacob had seen the Savior: "For he [Isaiah] verily saw my Redeemer, even as I have seen him. And my brother, Jacob, also has seen him as I have seen him" (2 Nephi 11:2–3).

That the younger Jacob was familiar with the premortal Christ is also attested by Lehi in a blessing when the patriarch acknowledged that this son born in the wilderness had "*beheld in thy youth his glory*"

(2 Nephi 2:4; italics added). That Jacob was well acquainted with the Lord is plain from his writings (Jacob 1:5–7; 2:9, 11).

Each Author Saw Our Day

The Book of Mormon was intended primarily for the latter-day inhabitants of the land. The Nephites had already been destroyed when the record was completed, and the Lamanites would have destroyed the plates had they had access to them (Mormon 6:6). The message of the book, therefore, is primarily directed to the latter-day "Gentiles, Jews, and Lamanites," as each writer was aware that his own people would not repent nor profit from his writings. They spoke specifically to us about their concerns. Mormon, living toward the end of the Nephite civilization, explained why he added the small plates of Nephi to his record without abridging them:

> And the things which are upon these plates pleasing me, because of the prophecies of the coming of Christ; and my fathers knowing that many of them have been fulfilled; yea, and I also know that as many things as have been prophesied concerning us down to this day have been fulfilled, and as many as go beyond this day must surely come to pass—
>
> Wherefore, I chose these things, to finish my record upon them . . . ; and I cannot write the hundredth part of the things of my people. (Words of Mormon 1:4–5)

In the book of 3 Nephi, we see that Mormon was familiar with our day because he bluntly chastised the latter-day Gentiles for their lack of spirituality and wickedness:

> Hearken, O ye Gentiles, and hear the words of Jesus Christ, the Son of the living God, which he hath commanded me that

I should speak concerning you, for, behold he commandeth me that I should write, saying:

Turn, all ye Gentiles, from your wicked ways; and repent of your evil doings, of your lyings and deceivings, and of your whoredoms, and of your secret abominations, and your idolatries, and of your murders, and your priestcrafts, and your envyings, and your strifes, and from all your wickedness and abominations, and come unto me, and be baptized in my name, that ye may receive a remission of your sins, and be filled with the Holy Ghost, that ye may be numbered with my people who are of the house of Israel. (3 Nephi 30:1–2)

Moroni, too, spoke plainly of our day and of the coming forth of the Book of Mormon:

The Lord hath shown unto me great and marvelous things concerning that which must shortly come, at that day when these things shall come forth among you.

Behold, I speak unto you as if ye were present, and yet ye are not. But behold, Jesus Christ hath shown you unto me, and I know your doing. (Mormon 8:34–35)

Moroni chronicled our day of materialism, clearly warning us of the conditions that would test the spiritual resolve of the Latter-day Saints while the Gentiles stumbled spiritually.

Nephi wrote, "The Lord God promised unto me that these things which I write shall be kept and preserved, and handed down unto my seed, from generation to generation" (2 Nephi 25:21). He saw the conditions of our day, and he cautioned those who would write after him that they were not to "occupy these plates with things which are not of worth unto the children of men" (1 Nephi 6:6). From what he recorded of his own experience, together with an extensive commentary on Isaiah (2 Nephi 25–33), we see that he knew the conditions we face in these latter days. Nephi detailed the coming of the Gentiles to this land (1 Nephi 12–15). He also knew, sadly enough, that the Lamanites would be the Lord's agent to sweep his own people from the land.

Jacob, who succeeded Nephi as a recorder, outlined the charge given him: "Nephi gave me, Jacob, a commandment concerning the small plates, upon which these things are engraven. And he gave me, Jacob, a commandment that I should write upon these plates a few of the things which I considered to be most precious; that I should not touch, save it were lightly, concerning the history of this people. . . . For he said that the history of his people should be engraven upon his other plates" (Jacob 1:1–3). Jacob, like his brother Nephi, quoted and commented on a number of Isaiah's writings that pertain to our day. He provided insights and observations concerning the state of the latter-day Gentiles (2 Nephi 6–10). One of his most perceptive comments was "this land shall be a land of liberty unto the Gentiles, and there shall be no kings upon the land, who shall raise up unto the Gentiles" (2 Nephi 10:11). That modern America has never had a king is in itself a marvel, given the political background of the colonists before their victory over their "mother Gentiles" (1 Nephi 13:17).

Enos, the son of Jacob, knowing of the charge given to his father by Nephi, indicated that he knew that he too was writing to future generations (Enos 1:15–16).

Summary

The prophet-scribes of the Book of Mormon were well qualified to counsel and warn us about what we must do to avoid the disasters that befell their people. Though much of what Nephi and Jacob wrote on the large plates would come to the attention of the Nephites and the Lamanites who would join the Church after the missions of the sons of Mosiah, the smaller plates were written and preserved only for the righteous who would receive the book in the latter days. Mormon abridged the large plates, selecting the information that would be of most worth to the people on the land in our day. He did not abridge the works written on the small plates by Nephi and those after him.

Mormon and Moroni were abridgers and commentators who had an urgent yearning to warn us of the pitfalls they could see in our day. Mormon explained his problem: "I cannot write the hundredth part of the things of my people" (Words of Mormon 1:5; see also Helaman 3:14; 3 Nephi 5:8; 26:6). Being limited in space and writing materials, Mormon could record only a portion of the records available to him. Having seen our day in vision, surely he would choose examples and experiences of his people and from earlier records that would be most relevant to those latter-day people. President Ezra Taft Benson testified:

> The Book of Mormon was written for us today. God is the author of the book. It is a record of a fallen people, compiled by inspired men for our blessing today. Those people never had the book—it was meant for us. Mormon, the ancient prophet after whom the book is named, abridged centuries of records. God, who knows the end from the beginning, told him what to include in his abridgment that we would need for our day. ("The Book of Mormon Is the Word of God," 63)

On another occasion, President Benson spoke of the writers of the Book of Mormon and explained:

> If they saw our day, and chose those things which would be of greatest worth to us, is that not how we should study the Book of Mormon? We should constantly ask ourselves, "Why did the Lord inspire Mormon (or Moroni or Alma) to include that in his record? What lesson can I learn from that to help me

live in this day and age? ("Book of Mormon—Keystone of Our Religion," 6)

Elder M. Russell Ballard commented on Moroni's seeing our day:

> Political unrest, warfare, and economic chaos prevail in many parts of the world, and the plagues of pornography, drug misuse, immorality, AIDS, and child abuse become more oppressive with each passing day. The media busily satisfies an apparently insatiable appetite of audiences to witness murder, violence, nudity, sex, and profanity. Is not this the day of which Moroni spoke when he recorded: "Behold, I speak unto you as if ye were present, and yet ye are not. But behold, Jesus Christ hath shown you unto me, and I know your doing" (Morm. 8:35). And then he prophesied of conditions of the world as they are today. ("Joy of Hope Fulfilled," 31)

We may have confidence in the integrity of those who wrote the Book of Mormon and of the record itself, as we read of the rise and fall of the people about whom they wrote and whom they sought desperately to turn back from destruction. Our task as Latter-day Saints is to learn from these inspired authors what we may do to avoid the tragedies that befell their people. We cannot disregard the warnings of these prophets, for God made promises to those who pleaded with Him to preserve a record for future generations (Enos 1:16–18; D&C 10:46), and He did not disappoint His faithful disciples.

"I told the brethren that the Book of Mormon was the most correct of any book on earth, and the keystone of our religion," the latter-day prophet Joseph Smith wrote, "and a man would get nearer to God by abiding by its precepts, than by any other book" (*History of the Church*, 4:461). The latter-day seer could say that because these writings are relevant to us. The record was hidden for many centuries. Having been translated once (into English), this text gives us a better record of the principles of the gospel than we have in the Bible because of problems with its translation and transmission.

5

The Covenant on the Land

A covenant is a promise between two parties whereby each agrees to abide by mutually acceptable obligations. The covenant on the land between God and its inhabitants is an everlasting covenant. The civilizations prior to that of the Gentiles were swept off the land when they broke their covenant with Deity. They turned away from the promises made by their righteous forebears. It is the inhabitants, not God, who seem to find it difficult, especially in times of ease and prosperity, to maintain a righteous course, and when they break their covenant, the contract is void. If repentance and retrenchment are not forthcoming, severe consequences are inevitable.

The Covenant with the Antediluvians

The covenant between God and the first group of inhabitants on the land is not as clearly spelled out in the biblical record or even in the Pearl of Great Price as it is with later civilizations on the American continent. We know, however, that Adam and Eve were given dominion in an area known as the Garden of Eden. This first couple fell from a paradisiacal, or terrestrial, state in the garden to a telestial environment after Satan successfully beguiled Eve. Adam, not wanting to remain alone when his wife made a choice that would mean she must leave the garden, joined his wife and therefore brought the children of God into their mortal state. They were forced to leave their pristine surroundings, their promised land (or garden). Though one of the penalties they suffered was to be cast out of the land of their first inheritance, their transgression was not in the same category as the sins of the later inhabitants of Noah's time or the days of the Jaredites or Nephites.

Our first parents did not willfully rebel against God and His laws as did these later people. It is true that they broke a law of God, but living in a state of innocence, they did not comprehend the consequences associated with the violation of the law given to them in their level of understanding in the garden (2 Nephi 2:23). Like little children, they transgressed a law in innocence that caused their expulsion from the garden. This was part of God's plan, wherein they could learn for themselves through the experiences of mortality and the use of their agency. They had never seen death before, and in the garden environment, nothing they did made them sick or ill. They knew no pain.

Thus, the Latter-day Saint doctrine of the Fall is that the change from immortality to mortality was known to God beforehand and planned for accordingly. The plan of salvation was first explained to the Father's spirit children in a premortal council. In that first estate, we all understood that the Fall was necessary, and provisions were made to negate its long-term effects by having a Redeemer prepared ahead of time. Jehovah was called and chosen by the Father—in anticipation of the Fall itself—to be that individual. All who have come to the earth sustained in that premortal sphere the plan to come to earth. The fall of Adam and Eve was necessary to bring all of us to a probationary state where we could obtain a physical body for ourselves, where punishment and rewards are not always immediate, and where we could learn for ourselves the differences between good and evil in an environment where opposites can exist together. Such was not possible in the premortal sphere, for there perfection reigns and wickedness is not tolerated (D&C 1:30). When Lucifer sinned by rebelling against the Father, he and those who followed him were cast out of God's presence (Abraham 3:27–28).

To attain godhood, each of us must understand the differences between right and wrong. The point is that the violation of the law given to Adam and Eve was not done in rebellion against repeated warnings and threats of destruction by Church leaders or prophets as were the violations by Jaredites and Nephites. The decision of our first parents to go against God's counsel was done in a state of innocence rather than a serious plot to overthrow the kingdom of God. And when Adam and Eve learned of the consequences of their decisions, they repented of their transgression and were forgiven by God (Moses 6:53). Nevertheless, they had broken a law, a penalty had been decreed, and they moved into a state of mortality as natural, physical changes took place in their bodies. Blood replaced spirit element, and death became the inevitable result of their decision in the garden. The good news was that now parenthood and spiritual progression were open to them, and they rejoiced together (Moses 5:10–11). They paved the way for us all to come to earth for the wonderful experiences of mortality.

Enoch

Enoch headed the next dispensation after Adam. That the land in which he grew up was a land of promise is mentioned by him: "I came out from the land of Cainan, the land of my fathers, *a land of righteousness* unto this day. And my father taught me in all the ways of God" (Moses 6:41; italics added). Enoch came out of a righteous heritage and background. But by the time he reached adulthood, the people were in a state of wickedness and the Lord called him to preach repentance to the people. By then, the ripening process was already well underway with many of the earth's inhabitants. The level of wickedness that developed among the people caused God to send Enoch to warn the people of their impending destruction if they did not repent. "Go to this people," the Lord commissioned him, and "say unto them—Repent, lest I come out and smite them with a curse, and they die" (Moses 7:10).

War was already raging between the righteous people and the wicked who were justifying their sinful behavior (Moses 7:13). Until the people of Enoch were translated, the division between the obedient and the wicked of Enoch's city became increasingly volatile. Those who were not translated with his people remained on the earth and were later destroyed in the flood in the days of Noah (Moses 7:33–38).

The Jaredites and the Covenant on the Land

The covenant between God and the land's inhabitants is most clearly outlined in the Jaredite record. After the cataclysmic event of the Flood, the land was prepared anew for the Jaredites: "After the waters had receded from off the face of this land it became a choice land above all other lands, a chosen land of the Lord; wherefore the Lord would have that all men should serve him who dwell upon the face thereof" (Ether 13:2). The land was prepared for the Jaredite colony after the scattering of people at the time the tongues were confounded at the Tower of Babel (Ether 1:3, 33; Genesis 11:1–9).

Moroni's outline of the covenant clearly reviews the blessings (Plan A) and cursings (Plan B) of the covenant. Plan A involves choosing gospel principles and the associated blessings and guidance from the Lord that come from such choices. If the inhabitants choose to live this way, they will be allowed to remain on the land forever. Plan B, on the other hand, becomes operational when people choose evil and wickedness rather than righteousness. Plan B leads to the destruction of the inhabitants when they fail to repent as their wickedness becomes more gross and offensive. Moroni wrote:

> And the Lord . . . would that they should come forth even unto the land of promise, which was choice above all other lands, which the Lord God had preserved *for a righteous people.*
>
> And he had sworn in his wrath unto the brother of Jared, that whoso should possess this land of promise, *from that time henceforth and forever,* should serve him the true and only God, or they should be swept off when the fulness of his wrath should come upon them.
>
> And now, we can behold the decrees of God concerning this land, that it is a land of promise; and whatsoever nation shall possess it shall serve God, or they shall be swept off when the fulness of his wrath shall come upon them. And the fulness of his wrath cometh upon them when they are *ripened in iniquity.*
>
> For behold, this is a land which is choice above all other lands; wherefore he that doth possess it shall serve God or shall be swept off; for it is the *everlasting decree of God.* And it is not until the *fulness of iniquity among the children of the land,* that they are swept off.
>
> And this cometh unto you, O ye Gentiles, that ye may know the decrees of God—that ye may repent, and not continue in your iniquities until the fulness come, that ye may not bring down the fulness of the wrath of God upon you as the inhabitants of the land have hitherto done.
>
> Behold, this is a choice land, and whatsoever nation shall possess it shall be free *from bondage, and from captivity, and from all other nations under heaven,* if they will but serve the God of the land, who is Jesus Christ. (Ether 2:7–12; italics added)

The Lord promised these righteous inhabitants freedom from bondage and captivity. It was made known to them that no other nation or people would take possession of the land as long as the covenant remained intact.

This covenant is repeated frequently by subsequent prophets in the Book of Mormon record. The inhabitants were reminded of the requirements needed to remain on this land. "And thus the Lord did pour out his blessings upon this land, which was choice above all other lands; and he commanded that whoso should possess the land should possess it unto the Lord, or they should be destroyed when they were ripened in iniquity; for upon such, saith the Lord: I will pour out the fulness of my wrath" (Ether 9:20).

The Nephites and the Covenant

The Nephites understood the provisions of this covenant because Lehi and Nephi had taught their families and descendants concerning its promises, its terms, and the consequences of breaking it. Even before they arrived in the promised land, the Lord told Nephi: "Inasmuch as ye shall keep my commandments, ye shall prosper, and shall be led to a land of promise; yea, even a land which I have prepared for you; yea, a land which is choice above all other lands" (1 Nephi 2:20).

Lehi, in one of his last sermons before his death, reminded his family of the covenant that exists on this land:

> We have obtained a *land of promise,* a land which is *choice above all other lands;* a land which the Lord God hath *covenanted with me* should be a land for the inheritance of my seed. Yea, the Lord hath covenanted this land unto me, and to my children *forever.* . . .
>
> Wherefore, this land is consecrated unto him whom he shall

bring. And if it so be that they shall serve him according to the commandments which he hath given, it shall be a *land of liberty* unto them; wherefore, they shall *never be brought down into captivity;* if so, it shall be because of iniquity; for if iniquity shall abound cursed shall be the land for their sakes, but unto the righteous it shall be blessed forever.

And behold, it is wisdom that this land should be kept as yet from the knowledge of other nations; for behold, many nations would overrun the land, that there would be no place for an inheritance.

Wherefore, I Lehi, have obtained a promise, that inasmuch as those whom the Lord God shall bring out of the land of Jerusalem shall keep his commandments, *they shall prosper* upon the face of this land; and *they shall be kept from all other nations,* that they may possess this land unto themselves. And if it so be that they shall keep his commandments they shall be blessed upon the face of this land, and there shall be *none to molest them,* nor to *take away the land of their inheritance;* and they shall dwell *safely forever.* (2 Nephi 1:5–9; italics added)

When we view the covenant as it is outlined in both the Jaredite and Nephite accounts, we see that the inhabitants of the land have many promises extended to them when they are righteous. They enjoy exclusive possession of the territory. No other nation will come and take their land away from them; it is to be a land of liberty to the righteous. Prosperity accompanies righteous living. God promises to protect His people from outside domination or subjugation as long as they maintain the provisions of the covenant. Righteousness and obedience ensure the continuance of the compact.

The covenant among the Nephites was given in the simplest of terms: "Inasmuch as ye shall keep my commandments ye shall prosper in the land" (2 Nephi 1:20). That was Plan A. They were also given the alternative, or Plan B: "But inasmuch as ye will not keep my commandments ye shall be cut off from my presence" (2 Nephi 1:20). Many blessings come through obedience; but punishment, a loss of revelation, and a forfeiture of political and economic blessings are the consequences that follow the choice of evil. These are blessings and penalties associated with the way those who occupy this land treat the prophets and their divine instructions.

The conditions of the covenant were repeated by subsequent prophets and writers. Jarom used the exact words Lehi had used with his family members years earlier (Jarom 1:9). By Jarom's day the Nephites had grown wicked and rebellious. Jarom lamented the bluntness that was necessary to keep the Nephites in line: "The prophets of the Lord did threaten the people of Nephi, according to the word of God, that if they did not keep the commandments, but should fall into transgression, they should be *destroyed from off the face of the land*" (Jarom 1:10; italics added).

Many were swept off the land at a later time because of their wickedness, as Amaron recorded:

And the more wicked part of the Nephites were destroyed.

For the Lord would not suffer, after he had led them out of the land of Jerusalem and kept and preserved them from falling into the hands of their enemies, yea, he would not suffer that the words should not be verified, which he spake unto our fathers, saying that:

Inasmuch as ye will not keep my commandments ye shall not prosper in the land. Wherefore, the Lord did visit them in great judgment; nevertheless, he did spare the righteous that they should not perish, but did deliver them out of the hands of their enemies. (Omni 1:5–7)

This theme of a covenant land and the need to remain righteous was taught to the people throughout Nephite history.[1] King

Benjamin, circa 124 B.C., reminded his sons of the need to consistently obey the commands of the Lord "that ye may prosper in the land according to the promises which the Lord made unto our fathers" (Mosiah 1:7; see also vv. 13, 17; 2:22). A few years later, Alma cautioned: "Thus saith the Lord God—cursed shall be the land, yea, this land, unto every nation, kindred, tongue, and people, unto destruction, which do wickedly, when they are fully ripe; and as I have said so shall it be; for this is the cursing and the blessing of God upon the land, for the Lord cannot look upon sin with the least degree of allowance" (Alma 45:16). The covenant on the land may be summarized as follows.

GOD PROMISES THE INHABITANTS

1. They may live forever on this land of promise (Ether 2:8, 12; 1 Nephi 2:1–5).
2. They will be free from bondage (Ether 2:12; 1 Nephi 2:7–9).
3. They will be free from captivity from all other nations (Ether 2:12; 2 Nephi 2:80–9).
4. They will prosper in the land (2 Nephi 2:9).
5. They will be the sole possessors of the land (2 Nephi 2:9).
6. They will dwell safely forever on the land (2 Nephi 2:9).
7. They will be kept from the knowledge of other nations who might capture or overrun them (2 Nephi 11:8).

THE INHABITANTS PROMISE GOD

1. They will serve the God of the land, who is Jesus Christ (Ether 2:10, 12).
2. They will keep his commandments (2 Nephi 1:9).
3. They will repent of any evil or iniquity (Mosiah 11:10–21; Ether 2:11).

The Gentiles

The Gentiles were led to this land of promise by the impressions of the Holy Ghost to Columbus, according to his own account, but the Gentiles were not (and still are not) aware that a covenant exists between Deity and the land's inhabitants. That covenant was not known until the coming forth of the Book of Mormon, wherein the requirements for living in this land are outlined. Perhaps because the Gentiles were not led here under prophetic leadership, more mercy is extended to the present inhabitants because the Gentiles as a whole are unaware of the Lord's requirements for living here.

Yet, the Latter-day Saints *have the responsibility* to make known to the Gentiles the elements of the covenant, if they will listen, because the Saints have been given the Book of Mormon and know of its message and promises. The Latter-day Saints have been asked to share the Book of Mormon message with the entire earth. This covenant between God and those who live here must be made known to the Gentiles before major judgments are brought against them. Alerting the Gentiles to the Book of Mormon message and the covenant on the land was a primary theme of President Ezra Taft Benson's presidency: get the Book of Mormon into the hands of as many people as possible, in part so they can understand the requirements and promises that pertain to this land and its people ("Book of Mormon Is the Word of God," 2–5).

The Gentiles Have Responsibilities, Too

Although the Saints have an important responsibility to warn the Gentiles, the Gentiles are not without some responsibilities and accountabilities themselves. These relative newcomers were Christians when they came into this land of promise. Most of the early settlers—Pilgrims and Puritans—were God-fearing people who carried with them the Bible. In fact, Nephi points out that this record was brought by the Gentiles who crossed the great deep (1 Nephi 13:29). The first settlers on the land were seeking religious freedom that was unavailable to them in England and on the Continent. They understood the Christian tradition and message of the Old and New Testaments. They shared a belief in Christ and His teachings. If they were not accountable for the specific covenant as it is outlined in the Book of Mormon, they were certainly accountable to live the principles of the gospel of Jesus Christ as presented in the Bible.

The Book of Mormon is much clearer than the Bible in explaining that righteousness must prevail in this land. Obligations go with ownership of the land. Nephi pointed out the promises and penalties (Plan A and Plan B) that the Gentiles should be aware of even before the restoration of the gospel and priesthood had taken place here. The Bible outlines both the promises to those who are righteous and the consequences and penalties that come to the wicked if the sons and daughters of God are slothful and careless in keeping the Lord's commandments (Deuteronomy 28–32, including chapter headnotes). But the Book of Mormon outlines the promises to the Gentiles on this land in much more detail. It outlines the role they play in assisting the Lord in gathering Israel (2 Nephi 10:8–11). An angel explained to Nephi the blessings that would come to the Gentiles if they hearkened unto the message of the Restoration:

> If the Gentiles shall hearken unto the Lamb of God in that day that he shall manifest himself unto them in word, and also in power, in very deed, unto the taking away of their stumbling blocks—
>
> And harden not their hearts against the Lamb of God, they shall be numbered among the seed of thy father; yea, they shall be numbered among the house of Israel; and they shall be a blessed people upon the promised land forever; they shall be no

more brought down into captivity; and the house of Israel shall no more be confounded. . . .

Therefore, wo be unto the Gentiles if it so be that they harden their hearts against the Lamb of God.

For the time cometh, saith the Lamb of God, that I will work a great and a marvelous work among the children of men; a work which shall be everlasting, either on the one hand or on the other—either to the convincing of them unto peace and life eternal, or unto the deliverance of them to the hardness of their hearts and the blindness of their minds unto their being brought down into captivity, and also into destruction, both temporally and spiritually. (1 Nephi 14:1–7)

Though the Gentiles are accountable for their knowledge of the teachings of Christ from the biblical record, they have the added opportunity to accept the message of the Restoration, which began with the Father and Son appearing to Joseph Smith, the coming forth of the Book of Mormon, and the establishment of The Church of Jesus Christ of Latter-day Saints in these latter days. The revelation that has come to earth in our day is from the God they claim to worship! Surely with the worldwide growth and influence of the Church, with temples in greater proximity to more of the Saints, with missionaries coming to their homes and walking down their streets, the increase of Church membership, and an edition of the Book of Mormon being printed late in 2004 by a non-Church publisher (Doubleday), the Restoration cannot go unnoticed. The light of Christ is given to all men and women (D&C 84:46), and that light will lead honest people, decent people, everywhere, to notice the growth of the Lord's kingdom. Hopefully, they will want to inquire about our religious perspectives and read the Book of Mormon. As President Boyd K. Packer predicted, "Those who now come by the tens of thousands, will inevitably come as a flood to where the family is safe" ("Father and the Family," 21). Many will be drawn to the Church in great numbers if we, as Latter-day Saints, do our part to live the gospel and extend its blessings to our neighbors.

Nephi indicated that a significant problem facing the growth of the Restoration would be priestcraft, where individuals "preach and set themselves up for a light unto the world, that they may get gain and praise of the world; but they seek not the welfare of Zion" (2 Nephi 26:29). This problem surfaced early in the Restoration, and it has been a major hurdle in our spread of the gospel. Joseph Smith learned that his report of the First Vision was not taken kindly by the professional ministry of the day. The message from the Lord to Joseph that their "creeds were an abomination" (Joseph Smith–History 1:19) cut into their vested interests as people were attracted to the new, fledgling, restored Church. Historically, the Saints have been a minority. Nevertheless, as the Church of Jesus Christ continues to come forth "out of obscurity and out of darkness" (D&C 1:30), as our missionary forces increase, as the Saints continue to become better known in government and business enterprises, and as we as individuals and families live gospel principles and keep the commandments, the differences between us and traditional Christianity will cause honest inquiry. As we listen to the Lord's prophets at general conference, read the scriptural record, maintain high moral standards, contribute humanitarian relief, model a righteous and attractive lifestyle, portray standards of decency and righteousness by which God would have His children live, we can yet have a powerful influence on the people of our day.

Jesus, in his visit to the Nephites, explained why the Gentiles were brought to this land. He said to those at Bountiful that the gospel would go forth from the latter-day Gentiles to the remnant—the Lamanites—of those to whom he was speaking:

> Therefore, when these works and the works which shall be wrought among you hereafter shall come forth from the

Gentiles, unto your seed which shall dwindle in unbelief because of iniquity;

For thus it behooveth the Father that it should come forth from the Gentiles, that he may show forth his power unto the Gentiles, for this cause that the Gentiles, if they will not harden their hearts, that they may repent and come unto me and be baptized in my name and know of the true points of my doctrine, that they may be numbered among my people, O house of Israel. (3 Nephi 21:5–6)

Mormon refers to members of the latter-day Church as those who "have care for the house of Israel, that realize and know from whence their blessings come. For I know," he observed, "that such will sorrow for the calamity of the house of Israel" (Mormon 5:10–11).

Summary

From the very beginning of this world's history, a covenant has been established between God and those who live upon this sacred soil. Gentiles, latter-day Christians (including Latter-day Saints), and others occupy the land at the present time. That there is a covenant on the land is clear from the writings of the Book of Mormon authors. Though the Gentiles are unaware of the covenant, they come from a Christian background and must be responsible for behavior consistent with the standards of the Christian tradition. Latter-day Saints have a particular responsibility to reach out, teach, and warn their Gentile neighbors of the consequences that come to those who fail to live a Christian standard of conduct.

6

A Nation of Law

When the Lord led a colony of faithful souls to the promised land, they committed to "serve the God of the land, who is Jesus Christ" (Ether 2:12). For people to be wholly accountable for their citizenship, laws must be put in place as a foundation not only for regulating social and economic commerce but also for holding people responsible for their behavior (Moses 6:56; Ether 7:25; Mosiah 29:15; D&C 101:77–78). Laws are designed to preserve order in the community and safeguard the rights of individuals by restricting or limiting inappropriate behavior and public demeanor inconsistent with commonly accepted community standards. Laws also prescribe behavior. It is a fundamental tenet of the United States legal system that laws apply equally to all individuals via the equal protection provisions of the Constitution. Recall the Lord's counsel to Moses concerning all who come into the promised land: "Ye shall have one manner of law, as well for the stranger, as for one of your own country: for I am the Lord your God" (Leviticus 24:22).

Laws enable commercial transactions and political processes to function smoothly when a reasonable amount of certainty exists that both parties will fulfill their agreements. Without legal commercial standards, for example, business and commerce would be chaotic and we would return to a barter system. Without a fair and impartial set of laws and the means to enforce them, dishonest people gain the upper hand and cause social disorder as we learned with the Gadianton robbers. Without obedience to a commonly agreed system of rules and regulations, civilization literally would come to a halt. The simple example of traffic lights illustrates the point. When drivers honor traffic signals, transportation moves with relative efficiency. The failure of drivers to obey such signals, however, drastically reduces the safety and efficiency of automotive travel. Too, laws limit the agency of those who are unwilling to abide by established standards of conduct. Sadly there are many who will not comply with or voluntarily sustain the principles of human order and decency, who prey upon the weak, the gullible, the elderly and otherwise disadvantaged individuals. Laws and the threat of punishment hold many immoral persons in check.

Among the Israelites, the law of Moses was the basic law that regulated temporal and spiritual matters. The law of Moses and the laws of Mosiah formed the legal framework for the Nephite society to function (1 Nephi 4:15–16; 2 Nephi 2:13; 9:25; 13:29–30; 25:24; Jacob 4:5; Mosiah 29:15, 25–29; Alma 1:14, 17–18; 10:13–14; 11:1; Helaman 4:21–22). When the Savior personally ministered to the Jews and the Nephites, he gave his disciples a higher law that transcended the old law of Moses, and that higher law was known to the Gentiles through the New Testament.

The United States of America differed from earlier civilizations on this land because many of the Gentiles who immigrated here came seeking not only religious freedom but political asylum as well. From their own background, those who settled this land were wary of a monarchical form of government. Though most were Christian by upbringing, they held to many doctrinal errors that had crept into

Christian theology during the great apostasy after the ministry of the Savior and the Twelve. They lacked prophetic leadership and inspiration and were deficient in doctrine because of an incomplete scriptural record.

The Bible translations available to the Gentiles were a "stumbling block" to them, as Nephi declared (1 Nephi 14:1). The Bible contains errors both from intentional tampering (1 Nephi 13:26) and from unintentional scribal errors and omissions. The consequences of having an incomplete scriptural record invited and sustained theological confusion. The division of Christianity into many different churches is the most compelling evidence that the Bible, in its present form, is insufficient to bring agreement and unity on saving and exalting doctrines of the gospel.[1]

In the First Vision, the Lord told the boy prophet of the problem with the sects of his day:

> The Personage who addressed me said that all their creeds were an abomination in his sight; that those professors were all corrupt; that: "they draw near to me with their lips, but their hearts are far from me, they teach for doctrines the commandments of men, having a form of godliness, but they deny the power thereof" (Joseph Smith–History 1:19; see also 1 Nephi 14:1; 13:32–41).

False teachings concerning gospel principles, covenants, doctrines, and ordinances abound in the theologies of the day. Teachings on the nature of the Godhead, postbiblical revelation, the premortal life, emphasis on grace solely to the exclusion of effort, the purpose of baptism, Church organization, ordinance work for the dead, marriage and family life, and a host of other doctrines were simply missing or distorted among the faiths in Joseph's time. False theological innovations, such as Calvin's predestination and Luther's rejection of works, together with the pomp and ceremony that came to be associated with Christianity in the Middle Ages and beyond reduced the Savior's gospel, in too many cases, to a set of ethics with false theological underpinnings. The teachings of men infiltrated and complicated the simple doctrines taught by the Savior. The common people, during the time we call the Dark Ages, had no access to the Bible in the early period of Catholic rule. A great number of sects were spawned because of doctrinal confusion that came from a variety of textual interpretations. No doubt many of the Founding Fathers of this nation, those who contributed to the ideas in the Constitution, did not actively participate in formalized religion because of the vagaries and confusion and contradictory teachings found in the Christian camp. Ministers preaching hellfire and damnation to instill fearful obedience did not appeal to men of intellect, those who sensed that the true God was not to be found in denominations that taught about purgatory and hell, that little children, without baptism, were damned. As Deists, many of these early founders were humble, God-fearing men who were inspired to work out the purposes of the Lord through the Constitution to establish this nation on a sound political and moral footing (D&C 101:80).[2]

The Lord brought believing Gentiles to this land to prepare it for the restoration of the fulness of the gospel. He promised Nephi that He would assist the Gentiles out of their doctrinal nightmare and confusion by having Nephi and his seed write the gospel on the plates, and He would bring that record forth as the Book of Mormon in the latter days (1 Nephi 13:20–24, 32–36). When the priesthood was restored in 1829, this last dispensation became legitimate when doctrine and priesthood authority were once again on the earth.

These early God-fearing Gentiles, as Nephi saw in vision, after defeating their "mother Gentiles" (1 Nephi 13:17) proceeded to fashion a government that has lasted into its third century. The Lord had His hand in this work, as He Himself declared: "And for this purpose have I established the Constitution of this land, by the hands of wise men whom I raised up unto this very purpose" (D&C 101:80). The framers of the Constitution were inspired to create a government incorporating a unique system of checks and balances. Having experienced firsthand the tyranny of kings and dictators in their homelands, our Founding Fathers were sufficiently wise to establish a legal and judicial system that allows for self-governance, a representative system of government in which the people have a say in electing representatives. The system entailed three branches: legislative, executive, and judicial divisions. The legal system encompasses courts, judges, and laws that give protection to individuals in a trial by a jury of peers with the right to appeal. This was a new legal enterprise in the history of mankind. The Bill of Rights was added to the original document, ensuring not only that the Constitution would be accepted by the people but that certain liberties would be preserved under the new government, liberties that had been ignored or trampled under by monarchs in the settlers' original homelands.

Laws among the Nephites and Mulekites

The Nephites established a monarchical form of government. Kings had ruled Jerusalem since the days of Saul. King Zedekiah was king over Jerusalem at the time the Lehites and the Mulekites left the capital city (1 Nephi 1:4). Both Judah and the tribes of Israel were immersed in a kingship form of government for centuries. Thus, Laman and Lemuel could accuse Nephi of wanting to rule over them: "After he has led us away, he has thought to make himself a king and a ruler over us, that he may do with us according to his will and pleasure" (1 Nephi 16:38).

When Nephi and his followers were forced to separate themselves from the people of Laman and Lemuel, the Nephites desired to anoint Nephi as their king. Nephi recorded: "They would that I should be their king. But I, Nephi, was desirous that they should have no king" (2 Nephi 5:18). Nephi knew the dangers and difficulties that come with an unrighteous leader. Despite his reluctance, however, the people looked to Nephi as a king and protector (2 Nephi 6:2), and near the close of his life, he did ordain a king as his successor:

> Now Nephi began to be old, and he saw that he must soon die; wherefore, he anointed a man to be a king and a ruler over his people now, according to the reigns of the kings.
>
> Wherefore, the people were desirous to retain in remembrance his name.
>
> And whoso should reign in his stead were called by the people, second Nephi, third Nephi, and so forth, according to the reigns of the kings; and thus they were called by the people, let them be of whatever name they would. (Jacob 1:9–11)

Having a monarchical form of government is not necessarily bad if the monarch is a righteous individual. We have positive examples of kingship in Nephi, Mosiah, and Benjamin and his son Mosiah. But the Book of Mormon also makes clear the damage a wicked king can inflict upon people. The pros and cons of a kingship form of government were explained by King Mosiah:

> Therefore, if it were possible that you could have just men to be your kings, who would establish the laws of God, and judge this people according to his commandments, yea, if ye could have men for your kings who would do even as my father Benjamin did for this people—I say unto you, if this could always be the case then it would be expedient that ye should always have kings to rule over you. . . .
>
> Now I say unto you, that because all men are not just it is not expedient that ye should have a king or kings to rule over you.

For behold, how much iniquity doth one wicked king cause to be committed, yea, and what great destruction!

Yea, remember king Noah, his wickedness and his abominations, and also the wickedness and abominations of his people. Behold what great destruction did come upon them; and also because of their iniquities they were brought into bondage. (Mosiah 29:13–18)

"We have learned by sad experience," wrote the Prophet Joseph Smith, "that it is the nature and disposition of almost all men, as soon as they get a little authority, as they suppose, they will immediately begin to exercise unrighteous dominion" (D&C 121:39). How dangerous it becomes for the governed when rulers seek power and control over others and surround themselves with cronies who seek to maintain their positions of power. Notice the parallels between Saddam Hussein and the people of Iraq, as Mosiah outlined the problem:

Now I say unto you, ye cannot dethrone an iniquitous king save it be through much contention, and the shedding of much blood.

For behold, he has his friends in iniquity, and he keepeth his guards about him; and he teareth up the laws of those who have reigned in righteousness before him; and he trampleth under his feet the commandments of God;

And he enacteth laws, and sendeth them forth among his people, yea, laws after the manner of his own wickedness; and whosoever doth not obey his laws he causeth to be destroyed; and whosoever doth rebel against him he will send his armies against them to war, and if he can he will destroy them; and thus an unrighteous king doth pervert the ways of all righteousness. (Mosiah 29:21–23)

When the time came for Mosiah to appoint a successor—his

sons were serving as missionaries to the Lamanites and therefore unavailable to assume the throne—a change was made in the form of government among the Nephites. Instead of a king, the Nephites created a system of judges elected by the voice of the people—by majority vote. Mosiah explained how this new order would serve the people best:

> Therefore, choose you by the voice of this people, judges, that ye may be judged according to the laws which have been given you by our fathers which are correct, and which were given them by the hand of the Lord. . . .
>
> Therefore, it came to pass that they assembled themselves together in bodies throughout the land, to cast in their voices concerning who should be their judges, to judge them according to the law which had been given them; and they were exceedingly rejoiced because of the liberty which had been granted unto them. (Mosiah 29:25–39)

King Mosiah acknowledged that the laws he ordained were of God. No doubt additions or modifications to the law of Moses were made by the Nephites over time through their experience (Mosiah 2:31; 3 Nephi 6:24–27). Suffice it to say that law plays an important role in God's plans for His children for, ultimately, laws make men and women accountable for their agency and behavior (2 Nephi 2:26).

Nonetheless, even self-government is not flawless, as Mosiah warned: "Now it is not common that the voice of the people desireth anything contrary to that which is right; but it is common for the lesser part of the people to desire that which is not right; therefore this shall ye observe and make it your law—*to do your business by the voice of the people*" (Mosiah 29:26; italics added).

When sensible laws are upheld and sustained by the will of the majority of righteous people, society functions smoothly. Even then, however, it may be difficult to find a unanimity of opinion on any particular issue. Righteous people may disagree or have different opinions on numerous issues. Both the Republican and the Democratic parties have members who are faithful Latter-day Saints. Varied opinions will always exist among constituents as to what government services should be provided and the extent to which people are willing to be taxed for such services. There has been, for example, a historic divide in our country between those on the so-called political "left" and those on the "right" who disagree over the amount of government involvement in community and individual affairs.[3]

The best course of action, the Nephite king counseled, is to make and sustain laws and policies by the voice of the people—the majority. When most of the people are righteous, sustain equitable laws, and elect officials who conscientiously sustain existing laws while the judiciary interprets the laws without regard to money or bribes, chances are improved for harmony in the populace. The principle is that if elected officials fail to uphold laws sustained by the majority of people, the next election will find the majority turning the incumbents out of office.[4]

King Mosiah also saw the weaknesses of self-government: "And if the time comes that the *voice of the people* doth choose iniquity; *then is the time that the judgments of God will come upon you;* yea, then is the time he will visit you with great destruction even as he has hitherto visited this land" (Mosiah 29:27; italics added).

Here is a key component! If the majority believes in and upholds strong, decent, and equitable laws, the standard of decency keeps society moving along. But should the greater proportion of the people become fuzzy about what is right and wrong and initiate or sustain legislation that encourages or protects the wicked, or when evil men and women or their legal representatives manipulate the system to avoid punishment or legal consequences for illegal acts, then a democracy can become as corrupt as that of a wicked kingship. The universal principle is that the rights and blessings of citizenship must be accompanied by responsibilities and accountability. When the majority of people in a society influence and maintain government processes and righteous leaders through the ballot box, then that same majority must be held accountable for those who are voted into office. We have learned by sad experience that the minority, even a righteous minority, can suffer as did the Latter-day Saints in their early history when the majority of people in this land and their leaders refused to come to their aid, ignoring the principles of the Constitution they had sworn to uphold.

The Breakdown of Nephite Laws

Early in the Book of Mormon account, Nephi was instructed:

> Inasmuch as ye shall keep my commandments, ye shall prosper, and shall be led to a land of promise; yea, even a land which I have prepared for you; yea, a land which is choice above all other lands. . . .
>
> And inasmuch as thou shalt keep my commandments, thou shalt be made a ruler and a teacher over thy brethren.
>
> For behold, in that day that they shall rebel against me, I will curse them even with a sore curse, and they shall have no power over thy seed except they shall rebel against me also.
>
> And if it so be that they [the Nephites] rebel against me, they [the Lamanites] shall be a scourge unto thy seed, to stir them up in the ways of remembrance. (1 Nephi 2:20–24)

Later, after the Lamanites killed many Nephites, the followers of Nephi were humbled by the losses they sustained. They understood that they had become lax in sustaining and maintaining the laws of God. The prophet-writer at the time, Nephi, son of Helaman, wrote this poignant summation:

Yea, they began to remember the prophecies of Alma, and also the words of Mosiah; and they saw that they had been a stiffnecked people, and that they had set at naught the commandments of God;

And that they had altered and trampled under their feet the laws of Mosiah, or that which the Lord commanded him to give unto the people; and they saw that their laws had become corrupted, and that they had become a wicked people insomuch that they were wicked even like unto the Lamanites. . . .

And they saw that they had become weak, like unto their brethren, the Lamanites, and that the Spirit of the Lord did no more preserve them; yea, it had withdrawn from them because the Spirit of the Lord doth not dwell in unholy temples—

Therefore the Lord did cease to preserve them by his miraculous and matchless power, for they had fallen into a state of unbelief and awful wickedness; and they saw that the Lamanites were exceedingly more numerous than they, and except they should cleave unto the Lord their God they must unavoidably perish. (Helaman 4:21–25; italics added)

When the Nephites trampled divine laws, laws that were designed to regulate and maintain order in their society, the people began to ripen in iniquity. They sought to introduce wicked practices among the people. Warned by prophets but refusing to abide by the laws that came from God, they opened themselves up to His judgments:

For as their laws and their governments were established by the voice of the people, and they who chose evil were more numerous than they who chose good, therefore they were ripening for destruction, for the laws had become corrupted.

Yea, and this was not all; they were a stiffnecked people, insomuch that they could not be governed by the law nor justice, save it were to their destruction. (Helaman 5:2–3)

Without swift repentance and reformation, the covenant on the land was fractured and the Nephites lost the divine protection of covenants with Deity. Physical and spiritual penalties came upon them until they were eventually destroyed.

The Disintegration of the Legal Framework

Except for the Lamanites, the Jaredite and Nephite civilizations were completely annihilated. The downfall of these two nations attests to the principle that the laws of God cannot be violated with impunity, nor can unrighteousness on this land be tolerated to any great extent without serious temporal and spiritual consequences. A study of these civilizations gives us insight into the state of the present Gentile civilization.

The breakdown of law among the Nephites led to wickedness, arrogance, chaos, pride, and a lack of spiritual vision. When the leaders who are responsible for maintaining and administering the law become selfish, greedy, and tainted by corruption, governmental processes quickly break down. Self-interest and self-preservation then dominate the landscape, and concern for the welfare of others is quickly abated. Interestingly enough, Alma singled out the group he thought most responsible for the decline in law and order and who persecuted the righteous:

> Now it was those men who sought to destroy them who were lawyers, who were hired or appointed by the people to administer the law at their times of trials, or at the trials of the crimes of the people before the judges.
>
> Now these lawyers were learned in all the arts and cunning of the people; and this was to enable them that they might be skilful in their profession. (Alma 10:14–15)

In the United States, when judges and lawyers interpret laws

73

consistent with the meaning of the inspired Constitution, society remains strong and stable. But when the very officers who are elected to safeguard and enforce sensible laws ignore them or use them to advance their own evil purposes, the law then begins to undermine justice, and it becomes a curse rather than a blessing. Amulek explained the outcome of such actions: "I say unto you, that the foundation of the destruction of this people is beginning to be laid by the unrighteousness of your lawyers and your judges" (Alma 10:27). When laws are disregarded or ignored or when those whose task it is to enforce the laws fail to do so—or even worse, when they manipulate the law for personal gain—then the law, no matter how inspired, cannot bless the citizens.

This problem of ignoring laws, or thinking one is above the law, was a major issue among the Nephites and one that led to their destruction. Though their laws had come from God through inspired prophets and leaders, the laws were broken or ignored when the wicked ascended to power. Because the laws originated with God, however, their violation could not occur without divine displeasure and warnings. The Lord made it clear to Nephi early in the record what would happen if the Nephites fell into transgression: The Lamanites "shall be a scourge unto thy seed, to stir them up in remembrance of me; and inasmuch as they will not remember me, and hearken unto my words, they shall scourge them *even unto destruction*" (2 Nephi 5:25; italics added). The story of the Nephites, as it unfolds in the writings of Mormon, attests to this principle. Society fell apart when God-given laws were disregarded with impunity.

The Nephites reached the point when

> their laws and their governments were established by the voice of the people, and they who chose evil were more numerous than they who chose good, therefore they were ripening for destruction, for the laws had become corrupted.

> Yea, and this was not all; they were a stiffnecked people,
> insomuch that they could not be governed by the law nor jus-
> tice, save it were to their destruction. (Helaman 5:2–3)

When God-ordained laws are trampled with regularity and the majority of people allow those in power to continue to use the laws to justify wickedness, then the people become accountable because they are the ones who voted for corrupt officials. Where people have the right to vote on their representatives (or judges, in the case of the Nephites) and they consistently vote in candidates who misuse the system for their own gain, not only do the people suffer from their lack of political involvement or choices but they elect representatives who jeopardize the covenant with God.

Application to Our Day

As American citizens, we have an important say in the quality of our political leaders because we elect representatives to serve in government. The Lord commanded us to seek for good men and women who will represent people fairly and accurately and be in harmony with righteous guidelines (D&C 98:10). As recipients of the blessings of self-government, Americans are also accountable for how the governmental processes work. It is our obligation as citizens to insist on reasonable laws and righteous legislators, and we ourselves must be willing to obey the laws. We can—and must—monitor and influence government leaders and processes by our participation through the voting process. By bringing men and women to office who will serve the people humbly and well, we safeguard the Constitution, our legal system, and our way of life. To the extent that we allow wicked men and women to remain in high places, we do ourselves a disservice and perpetuate an evil system that can destroy our way of life. The small proportion of people in this country who vote in most elections is a sad commentary on the interest of the electorate to secure righteous and God-fearing candidates.

To assess our collective performance as Americans, consider this question: Have the inhabitants of our land reached the point where most of the people are choosing evil over good? If not, then we will be blessed as long as the wicked remain a minority. If we have more who want to sustain evil rather than good, then we are in violation of the principle taught by King Mosiah: "*if* the time comes that the *voice of the people doth choose iniquity, then* is the time that the judgments of God will come upon you; yea, then is the time he will visit you with great destruction even as he has hitherto visited this land" (Mosiah 29:27; italics added).

Consider the issue of abortion as an example. Does a majority of citizens of this nation sanction abortion as a form of birth control?[5] If the majority agrees that an abortion depends on the woman's choice alone, with no regard for the sanctity of the unborn life within her, is such a decision in harmony with what the God of the land, Jesus Christ, desires? If a majority of people seek abortions in situations that do not threaten the life of the mother, are they violating the covenant between God and the inhabitants of the land? In its effects, was the decision of the Supreme Court in *Roe vs. Wade* a righteous decision? When wicked individuals gain a Constitutional right to perform or receive an abortion, is that pleasing to God? We each must answer for ourselves.

We might ask other questions: "Do a majority of people living on this land—the voice of the people, as Mosiah put it—accept the idea that consenting adults should be able to live together without being married? Can people live together or be sexually active outside of marriage without offending God and violating the spirit of the law of the land? Does interpreting or instituting a law that gives legal sanction to same-gender unions violate the laws of God? If most citizens support same-gender marriage, is that a violation of the covenant of God upon this land? In other words, does He care about such behavior?

The point here is that the Book of Mormon clearly teaches that the majority of citizens in a society cannot sustain wrongdoing or wickedness, nor can the majority pass or uphold laws contrary to the principles of the gospel of Jesus Christ without serious practical and spiritual consequences. When laws and punishments are enacted to prohibit crime, protect the innocent, punish the guilty, allow agency to function within sensible parameters, facilitate commerce within agreed upon guidelines, then there is safety in a free enterprise system nestled in a constitutional form of government. The opposite is also true. When there is evil, particularly among lawyers and legal officials, the common people usually suffer. As the Lord succinctly declared, "When the wicked rule, the people mourn" (D&C 98:9). Judicial activism, as it is called, has been rampant in recent years in this country.

The Lord explained the principle as it pertained to the redress of the Saints for the loss of their property in Missouri:

> And now, verily I say unto you concerning the laws of the land, it is my will that my people should observe to do all things whatsoever I command them.
>
> And that law of the land which is constitutional, supporting that principle of freedom in maintaining rights and privileges, belongs to all mankind, and is justifiable before me.
>
> Therefore, I, the Lord, justify you, and your brethren of my church, in befriending that law which is the constitutional law of the land. . . .
>
> I, the Lord God, make you free, therefore ye are free indeed; and the law also maketh you free. (D&C 98:4–6, 8)

Spiritual Laws

It is important to note another difference between present-day America and earlier civilizations, both on this continent and elsewhere: the fundamental principle of separation of church and state. Although as Latter-day Saints we believe that the Constitution and Bill of Rights were divinely inspired, we also recognize that the system of government and laws under which we live is not a theocracy but rather a collection of man-made statutes and institutions. Therefore, although the laws and regulations that a democratic society supports may be an indicator of righteousness for the majority of that society, it is important to remember that the Lord's judgment of both the society and the individuals within it will be based on laws and standards set forth by His servants, the prophets.

Judging from media accounts of unfortunate public scandals involving governmental leaders and other citizens, it seems that many individuals in America today believe that if their behavior (or that of their leaders) is not illegal, then such behavior is inconsequential and can be overlooked. Many consider that if a politician seems to be doing his job well and has high approval ratings, no one should care about the morality of his life. For example, the primary concern voiced during a recent scandal relating to the nation's president was the legality of some of his actions rather than the morality of them. When the Senate determined in impeachment hearings that those actions did not constitute "high crimes and misdemeanors," as set forth in Article II, Section 4, of the Constitution, the public seemed ready to let the matter rest. The danger of evaluating the moral status of an individual or a society in terms of legalities lies in the low standards of criminal law. Laws are in place largely to prohibit behavior so reprehensible that it must be punished by a forfeiture of basic liberties, that is, by incarceration or fines. Put another way, it is possible for an immoral person to conduct himself in such a way as to avoid prosecution under the law while living a life extremely displeasing to the Lord. Note, for example, that violation of most of the covenants made in the temple or at baptism or at marriage would not be a violation of the criminal laws of the land. The United States Constitution and many of the laws derived from it were never intended to be a moral compass but rather (in the case of the Bill of Rights) just the opposite—a barrier to governmental interference in individual moral behavior. Thus, the First Amendment does not directly promote religious activity, but it *prohibits the government from involving itself in such activity.* The Fifth Amendment does not require an individual to tell the truth, but it stops the government from forcing an individual to tell the truth if it will incriminate him or her.

Our personal standards and the standards of society the Lord allows us if we are to enjoy His blessings on this promised land are higher than the legal requirements. His requirement is that "inasmuch as ye shall *keep my commandments,* ye shall prosper" (1 Nephi 2:20; italics added), and "if they will but *serve the God of the land,* who is Jesus Christ" (Ether 2:12; italics added), then society will be free from bondage. No jury in the land ever convicted or acquitted individuals of violations of these standards.

Summary

When we observe conditions in America today and measure the behavior of its citizens against divine principles, it is obvious that we are slipping from our moorings of righteousness as we see a great effort to justify and legalize evil practices and behavior. The prophets of old knew that such inclinations would exist among the people if they became wicked and that such behavior would undermine the foundation of social order because of those who seek power and gain. "In consequence of evils and designs which do and will exist in the hearts of conspiring men in the last days, I have warned you and forewarn you" (D&C 89:4). Though the context of that warning is the Word of Wisdom, the application is also true that there are those who would use the legal system to extort, peddle drugs, form secret combinations, encourage prostitution, destroy marriage, lie, steal, gamble, and commit a host of other sins detrimental to the social order. The message of the Book of Mormon is that good laws must be firmly enforced if law and order are to function in welding a society into one of righteous unity. Integrity on the part of a nation's citizens leaves room to punish offenders while allowing for repentance and rehabilitation.

We must each, as citizens, ask, Are our duly elected legislators passing laws consistent with the will of God, laws that are in harmony with the principles of the gospel of Jesus Christ and the nation's inspired Constitution? Do the rich of our day consistently avoid prosecution because they have sufficient funds to find a prominent attorney who can get them off? Are the poor and downtrodden victimized by laws that do not treat them fairly? Are white-collar criminals able to avoid punishment because lawyers and judges can be influenced to find ways to free the guilty rather than seeing that justice is served?

The Book of Mormon prophets emphasized the need for the inhabitants of this land to be righteous, to sustain the laws of the land, and for the court system to administer laws fairly and uniformly. A society that will not uphold good laws will find it difficult to maintain peace and order among its citizens. As President Ezra Taft Benson explained:

> The fight for freedom is God's fight. Freedom is a law of God, a permanent law. And, like any of God's laws, men cannot really break it with impunity. So when a man stands for freedom he stands with God. And as long as he stands for freedom he stands with God. And were he to stand alone he would

still stand with God—the best company and the greatest power in or out of this world. Any man will be eternally vindicated and rewarded for his stand for freedom." (*Teachings of Ezra Taft Benson*, 656)

Our Constitution has served this country well for more than two centuries. It remains the envy of many in other nations who live under forms of tyranny and corrupt systems of government. Americans must remain committed to the principles that this inspired document embodies if we are to accomplish the mission God has given the people of this land and to His Saints in particular.

7

From Righteousness to Destruction

The ten stages through which each former civilization passed on its way to extinction are not difficult to see. The general pattern of moving from righteousness to total depravity and final destruction is fairly clear from the Book of Mormon accounts of the Jaredites and Nephites.

Stage 1: The Lord Leads the Righteous to the Promised Land

Adam and Eve, of course, began the first dispensation. After leaving the Garden of Eden, they settled in the promised land at Adam-ondi-Ahman (D&C 117:8). The Jaredites came to these continents under the leadership of Jared and his brother following the tower of Babel episode when God scattered the people and confounded their language. This righteous colony came by barges to the promised land sometime around 2200 B.C. Lehi was forced to leave Jerusalem about 600 B.C. because of the wickedness of the Jews who sought to kill him. The Mulekites, from Mulek the son of the Jewish king Zedekiah and contemporaries of the Lehites, came from Jerusalem when Zedekiah rebelled against Nebuchadnezzar (2 Chronicles 36:11–13). The Babylonian king killed the sons of Zedekiah living in Jerusalem (2 Kings 25:7); however, one of the sons, Mulek, avoided capture and death. The details of how young Mulek escaped, his exact age at the time, how many others were in his party, and how they negotiated the oceans remains unknown. When the Mulekites were found by the Nephites in the land of Zarahemla, "they had brought no records with them; . . . and [neither] Mosiah, nor the people of Mosiah, could understand them" (Omni 1:17).

Although these two groups came to this land from Jerusalem, they came by different routes, apparently: "Now the land south was called Lehi, and the land north was called Mulek, which was after the son of Zedekiah; for the Lord did bring Mulek into the land north, and Lehi into the land south" (Helaman 6:10). These groups were united under King Mosiah, as the Mulekites were taught the language of the Nephites and became part of the Nephite population (Omni 1:19).

The discovery of this land by Columbus opened the door through which the Gentiles streamed. Columbus credited the Holy Ghost for inspiration to commence his journey to the promised land.[1] Later settlers from England and the Continent came to this land because of the negative political, religious, and economic climate in their mother countries.

Stage 2: God Covenants with the Inhabitants of the Land

The second stage actually puts in place the covenant between God and those who reside on the land. Two options are presented to

the inhabitants. Either they will serve God and keep His commandments, or they will be swept from the land should their wickedness
sink to a certain level of depravity. The people living in Noah's day
undoubtedly were aware of the covenant (Moses 8:16, 20, 23–24,
30). The Jaredites were likewise aware of the promises on the land
(Ether 2:7–12), and the Nephites understood the covenant from
Lehi's teachings (2 Nephi 1:1–5, 9). The Lamanites were without the
gospel much of the time; like the Gentiles, they were unaware of the
covenant on the land. The Lamanites who lived in the northern
hemisphere later lost their land to the ever-expanding Gentile population (2 Nephi 1:9–11; Mormon 5:19). Sadly, all of these early
inhabitants broke their covenant with Deity. The fate of the Gentiles
is still in the future.

Stage 3: God Establishes Laws for the Governance of the People

In the third of the ten stages, God raises up wise men for the
purpose of codifying and systematizing laws so that people can live
in an environment of order and security and be accountable for their
agency. That is one of the problems Iraq faces as it gains sovereignty.
Establishing the rule of law so that society can function in an orderly
system is crucial for any nation's survival. If the rule of law cannot be
established, a nation may turn to tyranny, dictatorship, monarchy, or
tribal factions. From Adam to Abraham, the patriarchal order was
the system of government, and gospel law prevailed. Each patriarch
governed his own clan or tribe. The Jaredites operated that way initially. Later, as the population increased, a kingship form of government developed and a system of laws was put in place according to
the will of the king. The Nephites came to this land from a background of the law of Moses, which the great lawgiver received when

he brought the family of Israel out of Egypt. These laws sufficed until a higher law was instituted in the days of Christ. The specific laws by which these people were governed are only briefly mentioned in the Book of Mormon, but we know from the record that they had additional laws (2 Nephi 25:24; Jacob 4:5; 3 Nephi 6:24–27). No doubt other laws were needed to govern the people, as we learn from the record of Mosiah, which speaks of "laws which have been given you by our fathers, which are correct, and which were given them by the hand of the Lord" (Mosiah 29:25).

In the days of Helaman, much loss of life among the Nephites came because of their wickedness in ignoring divine law. Mormon, in his abridgment of the large plates, commented on this matter following a defeat of the Nephites by the Lamanites. He indicated that the Nephites had "altered and trampled under their feet the laws of Mosiah, or that which the Lord commanded him to give unto the people; and they saw that their laws had become corrupted, and that they had become a wicked people" (Helaman 4:22).

The Gentiles were blessed with a constitution, which the Lord "suffered to be established, and should be maintained for the rights and protection of all flesh, according to just and holy principles" (D&C 101:77). In the republican form of government the Founders instituted, laws are created by the representatives of the people through a system outlined within that inspired document. Judges in today's legal system are to apply the rule of law to specific cases that come before them based on constitutional provisions.

Stage 4: When Most of the People Choose Evil over Good, the Covenant Is Breached

When the majority of the inhabitants in this land choose evil over good, initial judgments begin (Mosiah 29:27). When people turn from a foundation of God-given or God-inspired laws to support or demand legislation contrary to that which is right and decent, and when the constituents uphold (and even promote) unchristlike practices or policies, when they vote for corrupt individuals who seek personal favors at the expense of the innocent or poor, wickedness prevails. Such evil practices became so widespread in the days of Noah that every man was evil continually (Moses 8:22) so that only eight people were spared death. The Jaredites were completely annihilated by a civil war that took the lives of millions of people (Ether 15:2).

When the majority of Nephites chose evil over good, their wickedness became a major factor in their being swept from the land. This matter of a majority making righteous choices is an important issue in modern times as the Gentiles of our day make choices inconsistent with the teachings of Jesus Christ. Nevertheless, at this point in the American timetable, there are still many decent and clear-thinking Gentiles who live here, people who, though unaware that a covenant exists on the land, are governed by Judeo-Christian principles of decency and law and who exercise fairness in their dealings with others. How long that level of decency and right-thinking will last as the proponents of evil gain an increasing hold on the minds of the inhabitants of the land will become evident in time.

Stage 5: The Lord Warns the Inhabitants When They Are in Danger of Being Swept Off

The Lord does not destroy His children until they have been warned multiple times concerning their spiritual laxness. God gives them ample warning through His prophets and missionaries when they are in violation of the covenant on the land. The Lord sounds a warning voice, and the people have a chance to repent. If they fail to repent, however, they become liable for their hardheartedness.

"And the Lord ordained Noah after his own order, and commanded him that he should go forth and declare his Gospel unto the children of men" (Moses 8:19). The Jaredites had ample warnings concerning their wickedness leading to their destruction: "And in the days of Coriantor there also came many prophets, and prophesied of great and marvelous things, and cried repentance unto the people, and except they should repent the Lord God would execute judgment against them to their utter destruction" (Ether 11:20). Among the Nephites, it was common for the prophets to threaten the people with destruction if their wickedness continued unabated (Alma 9:18; 10:18; 54:9; 58:9; 60:29; Helaman 13:10; 3 Nephi 2:13; 3:4). Alma privately told his son Helaman that "this very people, . . . in four hundred years from the time that Jesus Christ shall manifest himself unto them, shall dwindle in unbelief. Yea, then shall they see wars and pestilences, . . . even until the people of Nephi shall become extinct" (Alma 45:10–11).

How did these Nephites, who enjoyed political freedom, prosperity, and material blessings, move from a state of righteousness to a state of absolute depravity? Mormon labeled it "pride." He described the process among the Nephites:

> And the people began to be distinguished by ranks, according to their riches and their chances for learning; yea, some were ignorant because of their poverty, and others did receive great learning because of their riches. . . .
> And thus there became a great inequality in all the land, insomuch that the church began to be broken up. (3 Nephi 6:12–14)

Prosperity can affect people in a way that causes them to become critical of others, which is the antithesis of service and self-sacrifice, of humility and meekness. The Nephite record is replete with accounts of a prideful and selfish people (Helaman 3:24, 36; 6:17; 3 Nephi 6:4–5). Pride develops when people set their hearts upon riches and seek material gain at the expense of the welfare of others. Seldom do people acknowledge their own pride as a contributor to their problems, and thus they fail to see the need to repent. They can see only the faults of others, not of themselves (Helaman 3:1, 33–34; 4:12; 7:21, 26–28; 13:20–22; 16:10; 3 Nephi 6:13).[2]

One element of pride involves boasting about possessions, wealth, education, military might, or a lifestyle better than that of others less fortunate (Helaman 4:13; 6:16–17; 13:22; 16:12; 3 Nephi 10). Some people think that prosperity is a sign of personal righteousness. When men and women become self-sufficient, it is almost impossible for them to remain humble, to repent, or to take counsel from prophets who are warning them of their arrogant stance. When economic productivity brings financial prosperity, humility and meekness are often shown the door. Following the counsel and wisdom of the prophets is an important key to physical and spiritual survival. The Jaredites were destroyed because of their failure to follow the counsel and warnings of the prophets the Lord sent among them.

Problems often arise when greed and lust for economic or political gain come into conflict with the laws of the land—laws that are instituted to protect and prevent exploitation of the general populace. Unfortunately, there are those who strive to modify or change the laws from their original intent to justify wicked practices, but changing the laws to allow evil sets the stage for divine judgments (Mosiah 29:27; Helaman 4:22; 5:2–3; 6:23; 7:3; 3 Nephi 7:6).

When wickedness among the people increases, prophets and missionaries are sent to warn the people that their transgressions are violating the spirit of the law, the terms and conditions of the covenant associated with residing on the land. Judgments follow unrepented sins (Helaman 5:2–3).

When we look at the Gentiles living on this promised land, we see a country with unprecedented growth and prosperity, a nation with an economic output of goods and services that is the envy of many. With the accompanying prosperity and the pursuit of leisure time and technology, we must ask, Are there not abundant signs that we are mirroring the society of the Nephites and Jaredites? Are we not losing our spiritual moorings? Or have we learned to handle wealth, popularity, ease, leisure time, political freedom, and an elevated standard of living without becoming wicked and warped, as did the former inhabitants? Most thoughtful, observant people, in seeing the level of degeneracy in the media and music of this country, would admit there is a dangerous trend developing among us. The Book of Mormon authors warned the Gentiles of pride, the very thing that brought about the annihilation of the Jaredites and the people of Nephi (2 Nephi 28–30; 3 Nephi 30).

Stage 6: The Inhabitants Respond to the Warnings from God's Servants

Prophets and missionaries warn the inhabitants that their dishonesty, immorality, and selfishness are offending both God and the righteous who live among them. They are counseled to repent and reverse their course. If they continue to reject the warnings of God's servants to the point not only of ignoring prophetic counsel but of threatening the lives of those sent to warn them, they set themselves up for divine judgments of war, pestilence, and famine (Alma 10:22–23). If the inhabitants repent and maintain their humility as did King Benjamin's people, they reestablish the covenant with God (return to Stage 2). If people reject the message of repentance and salvation, the ripening process continues, and the sequence moves to Stage 7. If people simply tolerate the message of the servants of God, persecuting neither the messenger nor the message, the kingdom of God may continue to grow as more and more individuals realize that decency and integrity are antithetical to a permissive society. Destruction is delayed if people respond to the gospel message.

In the days of Noah, the people wanted no part of Noah's cry to repent (Moses 8:20, 28). The record of the Jaredites reads: "And it came to pass that the people hardened their hearts, and would not hearken unto their words; and the prophets mourned and withdrew from among the people" (Ether 11:13). Mormon lamented the outcome he knew was certain if his people would not repent: "I was without hope, for I knew the judgments of the Lord which should come upon them; for they repented not of their iniquities, but did struggle for their lives without calling upon that Being who created them" (Mormon 5:2).

Today, among the Gentiles, missionaries go forth in ever greater numbers. In 1974, President Spencer W. Kimball asked every worthy young man to shoulder the burden of missionary service. This was the first time in this dispensation that missionary work was pronounced as an obligation for worthy, emotionally, and physically stable young men of the Church. To ask every male at age nineteen to serve a two-year mission is an indication of the spiritual state of the Gentiles, not only in this country but worldwide. The message of the men and women who serve as missionaries is one of repentance, along with the good news that the gospel and the priesthood have been restored to the earth in these latter days.

Stage 7: When the People Reject Prophetic Warnings, the Judgments of God Begin

When people refuse to hearken to the warnings of those who are sent among them, judgments in the form of natural disasters—

droughts, floods, and a disruption of the food supply—begin. These penalties strongly influenced the Jaredites to repent. Such judgments deprive people of their possessions—homes and property—and force them to consider their obedience to divine laws and the level of spirituality as they must now depend on each other or the government. Such judgments naturally follow when the covenant with God is violated. If people will not repent, the ripening process moves forward steadily, and only swift repentance will save the people from destruction beyond this point.[3]

Prophets preach repentance and a renewal of covenants as the primary solutions to the loss of spirituality among the people. When citizens strive to change divinely sanctioned laws to justify further levels of wickedness, the righteous are called upon to declare repentance and to warn others of the coming consequences. The Lord does not yield on the requirements of righteousness necessary to live upon this land unless a sufficient number of people make an effort to change their lives to conform to correct principles. Amazingly, the wicked end up defending evil while claiming that God is satisfied with the way they are living! (Moses 8:21; Jacob 7; Alma 1:30).

Stage 8: The Spirit of the Lord Withdraws from the People

As people continue to reject the warning messages of the Lord's servants, they quickly lose their spiritual bearings. Evil becomes more appealing to them while righteousness becomes too confining. They are unable to discern between good and evil. They call evil good and good evil. When the Spirit of the Lord withdraws from individuals and society at large because of their iniquity, the "natural man" (Mosiah 3:19) surfaces, and carnality, sensuality, and selfishness replace humility and meekness. The inhabitants are thus left to their own greed as they wallow in filth of their own making (think of the effects of pornography). The result is inevitable contention and clashes with each other as competition and exploitation become the norm. Selfishness rules the day. Helaman observed: "And thus we see that the Spirit of the Lord began to withdraw from the Nephites, because of the wickedness and the hardness of their hearts" (Helaman 6:35; 13:8; Mosiah 2:36). Economic and political instability can break down a society into factions as suspicion and selfishness become primary factors in destroying both infrastructure and human relations.

Stage 9: The Inhabitants Become Fully Ripened in Iniquity and Cast Out the Righteous

We now see a society fully ripened in iniquity and good for nothing but destruction (2 Nephi 28:16; Alma 10:19; 37:28; 37:31; 45:16; Helaman 5:2; 6:40; 8:26; 11:37; 13:14; Ether 2:9; 9:20).

Each former civilization ripened in iniquity until it was destroyed. The term "fully ripe in iniquity" means that the wicked reach a state where they begin to cast out the righteous, the very ones pleading for them to change before it is too late to turn back. Helaman told the inhabitants of Zarahemla: "Yea, wo unto this great city of Zarahemla; for behold it is because of those who are righteous that it is saved. . . . But behold, the time cometh, saith the Lord, that when ye shall cast out the righteous from among you, then shall ye be ripe for destruction" (Helaman 13:12–14).[4]

In America, in the early days of our Church history, the Saints were cast out of their lands and ultimately cast out of the nation. They were driven from their homes, losing property and possessions. The nation paid for its wickedness by a loss of the Spirit of the Lord that resulted in a great civil war (D&C 136:34–36). At the present time, however, although our missionaries experience occasional physical assaults and derogatory remarks, we are virtually free to travel and proselytize in many nations of the world. It will be interesting to see what happens in the future concerning the treatment of missionaries and other Church members, given our growing numbers and influence in the Gentile culture.

Stage 10: The Wicked Are Destroyed

The Antediluvians were destroyed by the great Flood. The Jaredites and righteous Nephites were destroyed by devastating civil wars.[5] The Lamanites in North America were practically wiped out by the expanding Gentiles. When the warning cries of prophets go unheeded and the Spirit of the Lord is withdrawn from among the people, and when the inhabitants cast out or kill heaven-sent messengers, there is little hope for survival. When solemn warnings go unheeded, when the lives of the prophets are in jeopardy, typically the prophets withdraw and the people face divine consequences (Ether 11:13).[6] At this point, the land is cursed and the destruction of the inhabitants becomes certain. Though repentance is always open to people until their fate is sealed, at this point they seldom choose to cease their wickedness. When the spirit of repentance departs, when hearts are hardened, when people are fully ripened in iniquity, they stand condemned before God.[7]

As Latter-day Saints who understand these stages, we must continually ask, In what stage are the Gentiles? How slowly or quickly are they ripening in iniquity? What can we do to warn them?

8

The Fall of the Antediluvians

The Antediluvians were the inhabitants of the land of the Americas from Adam down to the flood of Noah's day.[1] This first civilization included three dispensation heads: Adam, Enoch, and Noah. Except for eight souls and the animals aboard the ark, however, the earth's population was destroyed some sixteen or seventeen hundred years after the Fall.

Adam and Eve

Adam and Eve and their family were the first occupants of this promised land.[2] Initially, the entire land mass was known as Eden, and it was pronounced "good" at its creation.[3] Later, God planted a garden "eastward in Eden" for His two children, and He placed them in it (Genesis 2:8). Had Adam and Eve kept the laws that pertained to their remaining in the garden, a place without noxious weeds or animals that inflict harm, they could have lived there forever. The transgression of Adam and Eve brought a great change not only to their physical bodies but to the entire earth and every living thing upon it. The two of them were cast out of the garden into a very different environment where they were forced to obtain food, shelter, and clothing by their own efforts. The good news, however, was that now the plan of salvation, the program we all sustained in the premortal life, became operational. The plan called for each of us to "leave home," our premortal sphere, to obtain a physical body as a counterpart to the spirit body we obtained from our Heavenly Parents. With this new configuration of spirit and body, we became capable of marriage and procreation.[4] The need for a Redeemer, for forgiveness, for agency, now became a reality. An eventual resurrection and return to Heavenly Parents as mature, experienced, married, resurrected couples, became a possibility, and thus we could carry out the intent of our creation as God announced to Moses (Moses 1:39).

After the Fall, Adam and Eve lived in a promised land, but unlike the Garden of Eden, it was not a paradisiacal environment. It was God's design that His offspring should carry out their probationary state in a location away from His residence where they could learn to exercise individual agency without celestial beings present, a place where they could learn, in time, to become Gods themselves.[5] This environment was to be a place where individuals, families, and society could freely exercise moral agency and prepare for their own future state of resurrected immortality and family life.

In contrast, when people live under tyranny, whenever unrighteous rulers or political systems operate to denigrate or trample agency, where oppressive measures are instituted by individuals or governments to thwart freedom, the plan of salvation is stymied. Our Father established the earth as a place where we could experience good and evil firsthand. We were given the opportunity to choose what we would do with our lives. Mortality had to be a place where God's children could learn the differences between right and wrong in an environment removed from their premortal home. Such an environment could not be located in a garden spot inside the pristine but sterile environment of Eden, where innocence prevailed. It had to be a testing ground where the curriculum of godhood could function. It had to be a place where law, choice, justice, mercy, and agency could operate in an environment conducive to growth and maturity, where the reality of death and damnation, eternal life and exaltation, were real possibilities. There also had to be an atonement to compensate for wrong choices and allow for a change in behavior—repentance.

The decision to move out of the garden to a place where the laws of life and death operated, however, had to be the decision of Adam and Eve. They had the choice to remain in the garden or move out into a hostile environment where the effects of mortality would be fully upon them. Had Adam and Eve not been properly instructed about their options and agency, they might have blamed God for the dramatic changes that took place once they were forced to leave their pristine garden. "It appears plain," said President Wilford Woodruff, "that it is God's purpose to suffer His Saints to be thoroughly tried and tested, so that they may prove their integrity and know the character of the foundation upon which they build" (in Clark, *Messages of the First Presidency,* 3:160). Adam and Eve put the plan of salvation into operation. The Savior made the Father's plan fully functional as He fulfilled the plan's provisions through His atonement, death, and resurrection, so that we too, as the children of Heavenly Parents, could become eligible for immortality and eternal lives (Moses 1:39).

The land we now call America was the location of the Garden of Eden and the site of the fall of our first parents. "Cursed shall be the ground for thy sake" the Lord told the first patriarch and his wife. "In sorrow shalt thou eat of it all the days of thy life. Thorns also, and thistles shall it bring forth to thee" was the divine penalty (Moses 4:23–24). "Therefore I, the Lord God, will send him forth from the Garden of Eden, to till the ground from whence he was taken. For as I, the Lord God, liveth, even so my words cannot return void, for as they go forth out of my mouth they must be fulfilled. So I drove out the man" (Moses 4:29–31). Moses recorded that afterward Adam and Eve "called upon the name of the Lord, and they heard the voice of the Lord from the way toward the Garden of Eden, speaking unto them, and they saw him not; for they were shut out from his presence" (Moses 5:4).

When Adam and Eve began their family, they taught the gospel to their children. They learned from angelic ministrants that a Savior had been prepared for them even before the earth was organized. They now comprehended the Father's plan, knowing that they were not to be cast off forever but could become candidates for salvation through repentance and obedience to God's commandments. As they learned of the plan and the provision of a Redeemer who would overcome the negative effects of their transgression and sins, they rejoiced. "Blessed be the name of God," Adam said to his wife," for because of my transgression my eyes are opened, and in this life I shall have joy" (Moses 5:10). Eve responded enthusiastically: "Were it not for our transgression we never should have had seed, and never should have known good and evil and the joy of our redemption, and the eternal life which God giveth unto all the obedient" (Moses 5:11). Being cast out of the garden was not, after all, a detriment to happiness and joy. It was not an eternal punishment or penalty, for their decisions were made there while they were in a state of innocence. But the declaration by God that they were to stay together as companions, as procreating partners, to begin a family was the foremost of the commandments. To that end, Adam joined his wife, and they were faithful.

Anxious to teach their children the "good news" after an angelic visitation and instruction concerning the plan of salvation, "Adam and Eve blessed the name of God, and they made all things known unto their sons and their daughters" (Moses 5:12). We must assume that "all things" means the plan of salvation and the knowledge that through obedience to God's laws and ordinances there was a way to overcome the consequences of their decision in the Garden.

But as most of us learn when we gather our children together, the devil is not happy with our attempts to teach our children principles of righteousness: "And Satan came among them, saying: . . . Believe it not." And as many parents since have experienced, the children of Adam and Eve "believed it not, and they loved Satan more than God. And men began from that time forth to be carnal, sensual, and devilish" (Moses 5:13).

The land where Adam and Eve and their family lived after they were cast out of the garden has been identified by prophets. President Brigham Young taught: "How our faith would stretch out and grasp the heavenly land where our father Adam dwelt in his paradisiacal state! That land is on this continent. Here is where Adam lived. Do you not think the Lord has had his eye upon it?" (*Journal of Discourses,* 8:67). Wonderful events took place in that first dispensation, and sad ones occurred, too. Cain's murder of Abel must have been a terrible ordeal for Adam and Eve. But a righteous posterity also came from these parents. Toward the end of their long life together, Adam and Eve gathered their righteous descendants around them. Jehovah appeared at Adam-ondi-Ahman to acknowledge the contribution of this first couple:

> Three years previous to the death of Adam, he called Seth, Enos, Cainan, Mahalaleel, Jared, Enoch and Methuselah . . . into the valley of Adam-ondi-Ahman, and there bestowed upon them his last blessing.
>
> And the Lord appeared unto them, and they rose up and blessed Adam, and called him Michael, the prince, the archangel.
>
> And the Lord administered comfort unto Adam, and said unto him: I have set thee to be at the head; a multitude of

nations shall come of thee, and thou art a prince over them forever.

And Adam stood up in the midst of the congregation; and, notwithstanding he was bowed down with age, being full of the Holy Ghost, predicted whatsoever should befall his posterity unto the latest generation. (D&C 107:53–56)

Enoch

The people who lived between the dispensation of Adam and Eve and the dispensation of Enoch were, in general, unfaithful to the principles and covenants given our first parents. We get a glimpse of just how wicked the people became during that thousand year period when Jehovah called on Enoch to declare repentance to the people of his day: "For these many generations, ever since the day that I created them, have they gone astray, and have denied me, and have sought their own counsels in the dark; and in their own abominations have they devised murder, and have not kept the commandments, which I gave unto their father, Adam" (Moses 6:28).

Though Enoch himself "came out" from a "land of righteousness" (Moses 6:17, 41), his ministry was not one of simply encouraging people to maintain right living that had continued down from the time of Adam. There was a need for repentance. The Lord gave Enoch his "door approach:" "Go to this people, and say unto them—Repent, lest I come out and smite them with a curse, and they die" (Moses 7:10).

Enoch did cry repentance. And in one of the few bright spots in the history of this world, a number of people began to change their ways. In time, Enoch established a Zion people, a people sanctified in the flesh, a people who were eventually translated and taken from off the face of the earth.

Noah

The removal of Enoch and his city from the earth left Noah with a difficult congregation. The scriptural account says: "The Lord ordained Noah after his own order, and commanded him that he should go forth and declare his Gospel unto the children of men, *even as it was given unto Enoch.* And it came to pass that Noah called upon the children of men that they should repent; but *they hearkened not unto his words*" (Moses 8:19–20; italics added).

In rejecting the words of Noah, the people of his day offered this logic: "Behold, we are the sons of God; have we not taken unto ourselves the daughters of men? And are we not eating and drinking, and marrying and giving in marriage? And our wives bear unto us children, and the same are mighty men, which are like unto men of old, men of great renown" (Moses 8:21).

The people did not consider themselves evil. They were blinded to their own wickedness. Doesn't that sound familiar? They argued that life was going on as it always had; they were marrying and having children, and society, to them, was not worsening.

Both Noah and the Lord knew better. "God saw that the wickedness of men had become great in the earth; and *every man* was lifted up in the imagination of the thoughts of his heart, being only *evil continually*" (Moses 8:22; italics added). When "every man" is "evil continually," and when the wickedness of the people has developed to such a terrible state of unrighteousness, their destruction is sure. People may believe that they are relatively righteous, that they are no worse than their neighbors. They may rationalize that they are as good as the next person. But when the Lord declares their wickedness to be odious and their days numbered unless they repent, the people have procrastinated the day of repentance beyond the day of deliverance. The iniquity of Noah's generation and their unwillingness to repent brought an end to this first civilization. Those who survived the great deluge included eight souls: Noah, his wife, and Shem, Ham, and Japheth (their three sons) and their wives (Moses 8:27; Genesis 7:18). Elder Mark E. Petersen, a member of the Quorum of the Twelve Apostles, commented on the survivors: "When Noah and these three sons, and the wives of all four, entered the ark, nothing is said about any children going in with them. Evidently none of their posterity was worthy of being saved from the flood" (*Noah and the Flood,* 23).

Noah used no anchor when the ark lifted off, and the vessel landed a great distance from its construction site. The huge land mass of earth, as it was created in the beginning, was still in one piece because it had not yet been divided into continents. That would not come until a century and a half later, in the days of Peleg (Genesis 10:25; D&C 133:24).[6] The subsequent settlement by Noah and his family after the Flood was in a very different land, far from American soil.

What a sad ending for this first group of inhabitants. To move from righteousness to annihilation is a terrible continuum. The people of this first civilization, greatly blessed initially, saw their descendants choose wickedness to such an extent that they lost the right to live upon the land. The ultimate penalty of death was administered to all but Noah's family. It was the worst calamity ever suffered by a people on this planet, as the lives of all human beings and animals were snuffed out, except for those within the safety of the ark.

Thus ended the first dispensation effort to bring the gospel and the priesthood to the children of God. One bright spot was the translation of Enoch's people, in which the righteous were spared in a dramatic separation from the wicked. The Saints were removed to a terrestrial state where they could serve God in other ways. Joseph Smith explained, "Now this Enoch God reserved unto Himself, that he should not die at that time, and appointed unto him a ministry unto terrestrial bodies" (*Teachings of the Prophet Joseph Smith,* 170). After the Flood, the promised land of America was again sanctified for the next inhabitants, the Jaredites (Ether 13:2).

9

The Rise and Fall
of the Jaredites

One of the most poignant examples of how a civilization falls is found in the book of Ether. The story of the Jaredites is especially tragic in light of the numerous times that the Lord sent prophets to warn them that they were bringing a curse upon the land because of their wickedness. In time they were cautioned that they would suffer "utter destruction" if they did not immediately repent. But they refused the counsel, and the entire nation became engulfed in a civil war that brought about their extinction. There were only two survivors: Coriantumr, the king of the Jaredites; and Ether, the prophet-recorder who had presented to Coriantumr the options of either repenting so that he and his family would retain the land, or, should he not repent, all of his people would be killed except him. Moroni abridged the record of the Jaredites for our benefit. He wanted to warn us, as latter-day inhabitants on the promised land, to beware lest we should repeat the same stages that destroyed the entire Jaredite civilization. He counseled: "And this cometh unto you, O ye Gentiles, that ye may know the decrees of God—that ye may repent, and not continue in your iniquities until the fulness come, that ye may not bring down the fulness of the wrath of God upon you as the inhabitants of the land have hitherto done" (Ether 2:11).

A Pattern of Destruction

One profound message from the book of Ether is the need to follow living prophets. When prophets of God counsel, wisdom dictates that people follow that counsel. Therefore, one way to view the decline and fall of the Jaredites is to observe this sequence that repeatedly took place among them:

1. *Prophets:* Prophets were sent from God to warn the people.
2. *Message:* The prophets delivered God's message which usually amounted to repent or be destroyed.
3. *Response:* How the people responded to the prophetic message.
4. *Outcome:* What happened as the people responded to the divine warnings.

This sequence of the prophets warning people only for them to reject the message is repeated six times in the Jaredite record. In the end, all of the people were wiped out through battles that took place up until Coriantumr, the last king. When the king ignored Ether's final offer to repent and humble himself, the die was cast. Moroni explained that it was the Lord who brought about their destruction: "And now I, Moroni, proceed to give an account of those ancient inhabitants who were destroyed *by the hand of the Lord* upon the face of this north country" (Ether 1:1; italics added). Let us now follow these people from their beginnings in the land through to their terrible conclusion.

Jaredite Beginnings in the Land

The Lord led the Jaredites to this land of promise following the tower of Babel fiasco and the confusion of tongues (Genesis 11;

Ether 1:33). In an effort to avoid the adjudication of the Lord who "confounded the language of the people" (Ether 1:33), Jared pleaded with his brother to ask the Lord for the following blessings for them and their friends and family:

1. "Not confound us that we may not understand our words" (Ether 1:34).
2. "Confound not" the language of "our friends" (Ether 1:36).
3. Perhaps He will "carry us forth into a land which is choice above all the earth . . . that we may receive it for our inheritance" (Ether 1:38).

The Lord granted these requests and led this colony "into that quarter where there never had man been" on their way to the promised land (Ether 2:5). "And they did land upon the shore of the promised land. And when they had set their feet upon the shores of the promised land they bowed themselves down upon the face of the land, and did humble themselves before the Lord, and did shed tears of joy before the Lord, because of the multitude of his tender mercies over them" (Ether 6:12).

The members of this colony multiplied and spread throughout the land. Initially, they were righteous, having been "taught to walk humbly before the Lord; and they were also taught from on high" (Ether 6:17). In time they became a large and prosperous population.

As the civilization grew, the people desired a king. The brother of Jared, as Nephi would later do, cautioned that such a choice would not be in their best interests (Ether 6:23, 7:5; 2 Nephi 5:18). Recall that King Mosiah, the Nephite seer who first translated the Jaredite record from twenty-four gold plates and knew the story of the Jaredites, warned his own people of the dangers of a kingship. Perhaps his counsel also came from knowing the wicked acts of King Noah, the son of Zeniff, as well as those of another King Noah among the Jaredites. It was under Mosiah's counsel and inspiration that the Nephites changed their form of government to that of judges, replacing the tradition of kings (Mosiah 29:38–39).

The Reigns of Kings among the Jaredites

Despite the wise counsel from the brother of Jared, the Jaredites desired to have a king to rule over them. Initially, no one stepped forward to fill the position. Finally Orihah, one of the sons of Jared, consented and was anointed king. Orihah and his successor son, Kib, were righteous rulers. Then a grandson, Corihor, confirmed the fears of the brother of Jared when he rebelled against his father and overthrew Kib and took him captive. While imprisoned (likely house arrest), Kib fathered a son, Shule, who "became mighty as to the strength of a man" (Ether 7:8). This son was sympathetic to his father's plight, and he organized a successful coup that replaced Corihor and restored his father, Kib to the throne.

In time, Kib passed the kingly appointment to his deliverer-son, Shule. Although Corihor repented of his rebellion, a son of his, ironically named Noah, tried to overthrow Shule. He succeeded in taking the king captive for a period of time, and would have killed him except the sons of Shule "crept into the house of Noah by night and slew him, and broke down the door of the prison and brought out their father, and placed him upon his throne in his own kingdom" (Ether 7:18).

Rebellion and mischief continued, however. Cohor, the son of Noah, successfully divided the people into two groups: "And there were two kingdoms, the kingdom of Shule, and the kingdom of Cohor, the son of Noah" (Ether 7:20). In a fierce battle, however, Shule killed Cohor, and the kingdom was united again under Shule's reign.

At this point, prophets of God raised a warning voice to the people that their wickedness was offensive to the Lord, that they were violating the covenant that allowed them to live on the land (Ether 2:7–12), and that divine judgments were imminent unless they repented immediately. This episode is the first of many in the narrative, as prophets were sent among the people to warn them that their wickedness was jeopardizing their continued habitation of the land.

The Days of Shule

EPISODE 1

Prophet(s): Unnamed, but "sent from the Lord" (Ether 7:23).

Message: "The wickedness and idolatry of the people was bringing a curse upon the land, and they should be destroyed if they did not repent" (Ether 7:23).

Response: "The people did revile against the prophets, and did mock them" (Ether 7:24).

Outcome: Before the people were destroyed, however, the king himself stepped in and preserved the right of prophets to travel throughout the land calling people to repentance (freedom of religion). In this case, before divine consequences were unleashed upon the people, King Shule stepped in to establish a law throughout all the land giving the prophets access "to go withersoever they would; and by this cause the people were brought unto repentance" (Ether 7:25), and "there were no more wars in the days of Shule" (Ether 7:27).

In this initial rebellion, the king intervened and issued what today might be called an "executive order" allowing the prophets freedom to declare their message of repentance and warning throughout the land. Thus the people were brought to repentance, and they survived this first trial.

The Days of Jared

Omer succeeded his father, Shule, as king, but one of his sons, Jared, stirred up a rebellion against Omer, taking him captive. This act enraged the other sons of Omer, who set about to free their father. They were about to execute Jared when he did "plead with them that they would not slay him, and he would give up the kingdom unto his father" (Ether 8:6). This bluff saved his life, but he did not repent. Instead, he coveted the throne, for "he had set his heart upon the kingdom and upon the glory of the world" (Ether 8:7). Jared's daughter devised a plan to recover the kingdom for her father with the help of Akish, son of Kimnor. Her plan had familiar overtones: "Behold, I am fair, and I will dance before him, and I will please him, that he will desire me to wife; wherefore if he shall desire of thee that ye shall give unto him me to wife, then shall ye say: I will give her if ye will bring unto me the head of my father, the king" (Ether 8:10).

Akish agreed to the plan to put Jared back on the throne, and he organized a secret combination to carry out the deed. However, the Lord warned Omer "in a dream that he should depart out of the land" (Ether 9:3). Jared became king because Omer vacated the title. Akish, having now gained a sense of power through a secret combination, decided to kill Jared so that he himself might ascend the throne. Internal dissent among the sons of Akish, however, led to his death. Omer was restored to his former position as king. Emer, Omer's son, followed his father on the throne. For the next sixty-two years, there was peace in the land as the people multiplied and prospered so that Lord "began again to take the curse from off the land" (Ether 9:16).

The Days of Heth

After generations of peace and tranquility, however, wickedness returned among the Jaredites as a wicked king, Heth, ascended to the throne by murdering his own father. "The people had spread again over all the face of the land, and there began again to be an exceedingly great wickedness upon the face of the land, and Heth began to embrace the secret plans again of old, to destroy his father" (Ether 9:26). Prophets were sent to warn the people of impending judgments.

Episode 2

Prophets: "There came prophets in the land again" (Ether 9:28).

Message: "That they must prepare the way of the Lord or there should come a curse upon the face of the land; yea, even there should be a great famine, in which they should be destroyed if they did not repent" (Ether 9:28).

Response: "But the people believed not the words of the prophets, but they cast them out; and some of them they cast into pits and left them to perish" (Ether 9:29).

Outcome: The government, this time, did not step forward to sustain freedom of religion, so the judgments began.

On this occasion the king refused to intervene in behalf of the prophets. "And it came to pass that they did all these things according to the commandment of the king, Heth" (Ether 9:29). Consequently, the judgments of God began in earnest as the prophecies unfolded. "And it came to pass that there began to be a great dearth upon the land, the inhabitants began to be destroyed exceedingly fast" (Ether 9:30). Poisonous serpents were set upon the people until they "began to repent of their iniquities and cry unto the Lord. And it came to pass that when they had humbled themselves sufficiently before the Lord he did send rain upon the face of the earth; and the people began to revive again" (Ether 9:34–35).

Peace and prosperity reigned in the land for a generation before Heth's grandson, Riplakish, came to power. Unfortunately, Riplakish introduced wickedness in the form of polygamy, whoredoms, and high taxes. He even built prisons to house those who would not pay taxes. The people rebelled against his high-handed policies and killed him. His son, Morianton, restored a measure of peace again among the people for several generations until the reign of Com.

The Days of Com

EPISODE 3

Prophets: "Many prophets" were sent by the Lord to declare repentance (Ether 11:1).

Message: The prophets "prophesied of the destruction of that great people except they should repent, and turn unto the Lord, and forsake their murders and wickedness" (Ether 11:1).

Response: "The prophets were rejected by the people, and they fled unto Com for protection, for the people sought to destroy them" (Ether 11:2).

Outcome: Com protected the prophets, and the judgments were delayed. Com "was blessed in all the remainder of his days" (Ether 11:3).

Com was a righteous king, as was his son Shiblom. One of Shiblom's brothers, however, was a troublemaker and rebelled against Shiblom. He caused that "all the prophets who prophesied of the destruction of the people should be put to death" (Ether 11:5). Thus "there began to be an exceedingly great war in all the land" (Ether 11:4). Moroni recorded that the words of the prophets were fulfilled:

> There was great calamity in all the land, for they had testified that a great curse should come upon the land, and also upon the people, and that there should be a great destruction among them, such an one as never had been upon the face of the earth, and their bones should become as heaps of earth upon the face of the land except they should repent of their wickedness.
>
> And they hearkened not unto the voice of the Lord, because

of their wicked combinations; wherefore, there began to be wars and contentions in all the land, and also many famines and pestilences, inasmuch that there was a great destruction, such an one as never had been known upon the face of the earth; and all this came to pass in the days of Shiblom (Ether 11:6–7; italics added).

This great destruction resulted in "heaps" of bodies upon the earth, "and the people began to repent of their iniquity; and inasmuch as they did the Lord did have mercy on them" (Ether 11:8). The Jaredites, in this episode, were spared any further losses.

The Days of Ethem

Three generations later, a wicked king by the name of Ethem came to power.

EPISODE 4

Prophets: "In the days of Ethem there came many prophets, and prophesied again unto the people" (Ether 11:12).

Message: "They did prophesy that the Lord would utterly destroy them from off the face of the earth except they repented of their iniquities" (Ether 11:12).

Response: "The people hardened their hearts, and would not hearken unto their words; and the prophets mourned and withdrew from among the people" (Ether 11:13).

Outcome: With the prophets silenced, the Lord withdrew His spirit from the people. A series of wars began to decimate the inhabitants. The Lord provided numerous opportunities for the people to repent and change their ways, but they would not.

The Days of Coriantor

A series of political struggles ensued, and war came again. Moron was taken captive, but he begat a son while in captivity, whom he named Coriantor (the father of Ether), who also spent his days in confinement.

EPISODE 5

Prophets: "In the days of Coriantor there also came many prophets" (Ether 11:20).

Message: The prophets "prophesied of great and marvelous things, and cried repentance unto the people, and except they should repent the Lord God would execute judgment against them to their utter destruction; and that the Lord God would send or bring forth another people to possess the land, by his power, after the manner by which he brought their fathers" (Ether 11:20–21).

Response: "And they did reject all the words of the prophets, because of their secret society and wicked abominations" (Ether 11:22).

Outcome: This prophecy of utter destruction was carried out in the days of the prophet Ether and the king Coriantumr.

While a captive, Coriantor fathered Ether, the prophet-writer of the Jaredite record. Although Ether should rightfully have been the king, his grandfather, Moron, had been deposed by some unnamed "descendant of the brother of Jared" (Ether 11:17) and his own father, Coriantor, was held captive. This usurper may have been Coriantumr's father or grandfather, because "the days of Ether were in the days of Coriantumr; and Coriantumr was king over all the land" (Ether 12:1).

Ether "did cry from the morning, even until the going down of the sun, exhorting the people to believe in God unto repentance lest they should be destroyed" (Ether 12:3). His message was powerful, for he truly told them of all things, from the beginning of man; and that after the waters had receded from off the face of this land it became a choice land above all other lands, a chosen land of the Lord; wherefore the Lord would have that all men should serve him who dwell upon the face thereof;

And that it was the place of the New Jerusalem, which should come down out of heaven, and the holy sanctuary of the Lord.

Behold, Ether saw the days of Christ, and he spake concerning a New Jerusalem upon this land. (Ether 13:2–4)

The people rejected Ether's message and "esteemed him as naught, and cast him out; and he hid himself in the cavity of a rock by day, and by night he went forth viewing the things which should come upon the people" (Ether 13:13).

Many sought to wrest the kingdom from Coriantumr. There was constant warfare, yet the people refused to repent and humble themselves. At one point, the Lord told Ether to go directly to Coriantumr and explain his options to save his life and the lives of his family and followers or they would all be killed except Coriantumr.

EPISODE 6

Prophet: Ether, son of Coriantor.

Message: "Prophesy unto Coriantumr that, if he would repent, and all his household, the Lord would give unto him his kingdom and spare the people—Otherwise they should be destroyed, and all his household save it were himself. And he should only live to see the fulfilling of the prophecies which had been spoken concerning another people receiving the land for their inheritance; and Coriantumr should receive a burial by them; and every soul should be destroyed save it were Coriantumr" (Ether 13:20–21).

Response: "Coriantumr repented not, neither his household, neither the people; and the wars ceased not; and they sought to kill

Ether, but he fled from before them and hid again in the cavity of the rock" (Ether 13:22).

Outcome: The annihilation of the Jaredite civilization— Coriantumr and Ether were the only survivors.

Ether's Prophecy

Ether's prophecy to Coriantumr becomes a remarkable example of how prophets are able to see the end from the beginning, how they can give inspired utterances long before any details of the later events can be known. The extent of this prophecy by Ether becomes evident as we follow Coriantumr through to the end of his life and view how improbable the fulfillment of Ether's prediction was at the time he confronted the king with the details of the future outcome.

To illustrate the implausibility of Ether's prophecy that Coriantumr should be the only survivor of his civilization, we learn from the record that Coriantumr should have died numerous times from wounds and a loss of blood if not from infection (Ether 13:31; 14:12, 30; 15:9). But Ether's word was true, and the prediction was that Coriantumr would outlive everyone else in his kingdom and he would live long enough to see another people inhabit the land (Ether 13:20–21). Ether predicted that this people who discovered Coriantumr, would also bury him.

The profound magnitude of Ether's prediction deepens as Coriantumr battled his chief antagonist, Shiz. In an earlier battle, Coriantumr had killed Lib, Shiz's brother. Shiz was so enraged that he swore he would avenge his brother's death. This became the driving force in Shiz's insane effort to kill Coriantumr. Their armies were engaged in constant warfare. After one battle, Moroni wrote:

> When Coriantumr had recovered of his wounds, he began
> to remember the words which Ether had spoken unto him.

He saw that there had been slain by the sword already nearly two millions of his people, and he began to sorrow in his heart; yea, there had been slain two millions of mighty men, and also their wives and their children.

He began to repent of the evil which he had done; he began to remember the words which had been spoken by the mouth of all the prophets, and he saw them that they were fulfilled thus far, every whit; and his soul mourned and refused to be comforted. (Ether 15:1–3)

Battle Casualties

Millions of people died before Coriantumr realized that what Ether had told him years earlier was true. But now it was too late. To provide perspective to the extent of the slaughter among Coriantumr's people, we recall that when Ether first approached him with a solution to save his family and people, Coriantumr presided over a kingdom that must have numbered at least six to eight million inhabitants (Ether 15:2). In those days, people fought at close-range, hand-to-hand combat, in which a person was killed by a sword or blow to the head so that death came by bleeding or from a bashed skull. This is in contrast to modern impersonal warfare of death and destruction. In comparison with the millions killed in the final Jaredite struggles, from the Revolutionary War through the Vietnam conflict (including the Civil War), approximately 652,769 Americans died on the battlefield (*World Almanac*, 698).

The Fulfillment of Ether's Prophecy

Thus at the time Ether initially approached Coriantumr to deliver his ultimatum, Coriantumr might easily have scoffed at

Ether's prediction that all of his people would be killed except for him, because of the sheer size of his kingdom. To think that all of the inhabitants of the land could be killed before the king's death, given the fact that Coriantumr probably led his troops into battle, would no doubt seem preposterous to the ruler. And, there were times when it seemed that Ether's prophecy simply could not be fulfilled. For example, at one point the record states that his antagonist, "Shared, . . . also gave battle unto Coriantumr; and he did beat him, insomuch that . . . he did bring him into captivity" (Ether 13:23). For some reason, however, Coriantumr was not killed at that time. Coriantumr's sons retook the kingdom by beating Shared and restoring the kingdom to their father. Coriantumr and Shared later fought again; before Coriantumr finally killed Shared, the record states: "Shared wounded Coriantumr in his thigh, that he did not go to battle again for the space of two years" (Ether 13:31).

On another occasion, Coriantumr fought against Lib, who "did smite upon his arm that he was wounded" (Ether 14:12). When the king recovered from this wound, he killed Lib. Then Lib's brother Shiz swore that he would avenge his brother's blood and he "pursued after Coriantumr, and he did overthrow many cities, and he did slay both women and children, and he did burn the cities. And there went up a fear of Shiz throughout all the land" (Ether 14:17–18).

Shiz was so barbaric in his treatment of the inhabitants that many people fled to his camp in order to escape death, believing that he would conquer Coriantumr—for Shiz had "sworn to avenge himself upon Coriantumr of the blood of his brother." Somehow Shiz learned that Ether had promised Coriantumr that the king "should not fall by the sword" (Ether 14:24) which made Shiz even more determined to kill the king. He was not going to let this prophecy come to pass. In one of the last battles, "Shiz smote upon Coriantumr that he gave him many deep wounds; and Coriantumr, having lost his blood, fainted, and was carried away as though he were dead" (Ether 14:30). Shiz must have thought he killed Coriantumr; otherwise, he would have finished the deed at that time. But Coriantumr recovered to fight another day.

Coriantumr Sues for Peace

The ensuing battles became so fierce that Coriantumr "wrote an epistle unto Shiz, desiring him that he would spare the people, and he would give up the kingdom for the sake of the lives of the people" (Ether 15:4). But Shiz's condition for peace was that Coriantumr "would give himself up, that he [Shiz] might slay him with his own sword, that he would spare the lives of the people" (Ether 15:5). This demand angered the soldiers of Coriantumr, and they refused to surrender. Battles continued to rage. Again the king was able to escape, because when he "saw that he was about to fall he fled again before the people of Shiz" (Ether 15:7).

The Final Battle

As Coriantumr saw his people decimated, he wrote a second epistle to Shiz offering him the kingdom if he would simply cease to fight. But Shiz would not. The record says, "And on the morrow they fought again; and when the night came they had all fallen by the sword save it were fifty and two of the people of Coriantumr, and sixty and nine of the people of Shiz" (Ether 15:23). Following the next day's battle, there were only "thirty and two of the people of Shiz, and twenty and seven of the people of Coriantumr" (Ether 15:25). The battle ended when only two antagonists were left standing. Moroni details the end:

When they had all fallen by the sword, save it were

117

Coriantumr and Shiz, behold Shiz had fainted with the loss of blood.

And it came to pass that when Coriantumr had leaned upon his sword, that he rested a little, he smote off the head of Shiz.

And it came to pass that after he had smitten off the head of Shiz, that Shiz raised upon his hands and fell; and after that he had struggled for breath, he died.

And it came to pass that Coriantumr fell to the earth, and became as if he had no life. (Ether 15:29–32)

After the death of Shiz, Ether "went forth, and beheld that the words of the Lord had all been fulfilled" (Ether 15:33). His remarkable prophecy, uttered many years earlier, was now complete. True to the prophecy, the people of Zarahemla found Coriantumr, who "dwelt with them for the space of nine moons" before his death (Omni 1:21).

The Jaredites had many opportunities to repent and turn their civilization around in order to avoid the judgments that eventually destroyed them. From the beginning, they had been warned that "this is a land which is choice above all other lands; wherefore he that doth possess it shall serve God or shall be swept off; for it is the everlasting decree of God. And it is not until the fulness of iniquity among the children of the land, that they are swept off" (Ether 2:10). Many prophets warned of their impending doom, but they refused to repent and "serve the God of the land." (Ether 2:12). Thus a great people were brought to an end because they refused to follow the counsel of the Lord's prophets.

A Message for Our Day

Moroni saw our day in vision (Mormon 8:34–35). His people, much like those of Ether's, were destroyed. He felt impressed to point out parallels between his own people, the Jaredites, and the Gentiles who would inhabit the Americas. He pleaded for us to "repent, and not continue in your iniquities until the fulness come, that ye may not bring down the fulness of the wrath of God upon you *as the inhabitants of the land have hitherto done*" (Ether 2:11; italics added).

As the latter-day occupants of the promised land, we face a similar test of following God's prophets. Because this promise was extended to those who inhabited the land "from that time henceforth and forever" (Ether 2:8), if we will not follow our inspired leaders, then we will suffer the same fate as did these Jaredites.

We are to heed the prophets in our own day. The Lord organized His Church and kingdom with a First Presidency and Quorum of Twelve Apostles, with each member sustained by the membership as a prophet, seer, and revelator. Every six months, our leaders counsel and warn us on how we may improve our lives and avoid the tragedies that came to these earlier inhabitants.

Summary

The principle of following God's prophets has always been a test of discipleship for the children of God. Establishing a community of the pure in heart can only come when individuals accept direction from living prophets. Our destiny as individuals in this dispensation, as it was for the Nephites and Jaredites, will be influenced by our willingness to listen to and heed the counsel of our living prophets.

President Wilford Woodruff warned the Latter-day Saints:

> We, as a people, should not treat lightly this counsel, for I will tell you in the name of the Lord—and I have watched it from the time I became a member of this Church—there is no man who undertakes to run counter to the counsel of the legally authorized leader of this people that ever prospers, and

no such man ever will prosper. . . . You will find that all persons who take a stand against this counsel will never prosper. . . . When counsel comes we should not treat it lightly, *no matter to what subject it pertains,* for if we do, it will work evil unto us. (*Journal of Discourses,* 14:33; italics added)

In a general conference address, Elder M. Russell Ballard promised the Saints:

Today I make you a promise. It's a simple one, but it is true. If you will listen to the living prophet and the apostles and heed our counsel, you will not go astray. . . . I promise you in the name of the Lord that if you will listen not just with your ears but also with your heart, the Holy Ghost will manifest the truth unto you of the messages delivered by President Hinckley, his counselors, the Apostles, and other leaders of the Church. ("His Word Ye Shall Receive," 66–67)

10

The Rise and Fall of the Nephites and Mulekites

Most of the Book of Mormon record deals with the Nephite civilization, which included the Mulekites. By examining the stages through which those civilizations passed, we can look at the Gentile nations to which we belong to more easily identify the stages through which we are passing. If we understand these stages, we may more readily comprehend the message that Mormon and Moroni left us. Likewise, we need to understand the counsel of prophets in our own day so that we may avoid the same tragedies that plagued these earlier civilizations.

Stage 1: The Lord Leads Lehi and His Family to the Promised Land

The story of Lehi and his family, the account that begins the Book of Mormon record as we have it,[1] is, like the other civilizations that have inhabited this land, one of joy and sadness. As we read the account of the family leaving Jerusalem, we are saddened by the choices made by the two eldest brothers, Laman and Lemuel. Through their behavior, we see how poor decisions over time can affect a large number of people. These two brothers became enemies to the truth while Nephi, Sam, Zoram, and their companions remained faithful to the counsel of Lehi and the commands of God. The behavior of Laman and Lemuel is somewhat ironic, considering that Zoram, someone outside Lehi's immediate family, became one of the faithful followers of Nephi and the Lord. We are reminded that this is the case in many families, in which souls become lost to the truths of the gospel because of the hardships of mortality. Laman and Lemuel should have known better, should have been stalwarts, but they could not see past the physical difficulties of the journey and allowed themselves to fall away from the gospel their father and brother taught.

Lehi was commanded to leave Jerusalem because of death threats from the Jews. "And it came to pass that the Jews did mock him because of the things which he testified of them; for he truly testified of their wickedness and their abominations; . . . and they also sought his life, that they might take it away" (1 Nephi 1:19–20). Having been warned by the Lord in a dream "that he should take his family and depart into the wilderness," Lehi left behind the comforts of home, and with his family headed for the borders of the Red Sea (1 Nephi 2:2). Lehi later reminisced about the difficult journey, yet he rejoiced that they had "obtained a land of promise, a land which is choice above all other lands; a land which the Lord Goth hath covenanted with me should be a land for the inheritance of my seed. Yea, the Lord hath covenanted this land unto me, and to my children forever" (2 Nephi 1:5).

Nephi wrote of a similar promise to him: "Blessed art thou, Nephi, because of thy faith, for thou hast sought me diligently, with lowliness of heart. And inasmuch as ye shall keep my commandments, ye shall prosper, and shall be led to a land of promise; yea, even a land which I have prepared for you; yea, a land which is choice above all other lands" (1 Nephi 2:19–20). After an eventful and arduous venture, the colony reached the promised land.

Stage 2: God Covenants with the Inhabitants of the Land

The covenant between God and the Nephites was the same as that of the Antediluvians and the Jaredites. The covenant was prefigured by Nephi long before they reached the promised land: "I remembered the words of the Lord which he spake unto me in the wilderness, saying that: Inasmuch as thy seed shall keep my commandments, they shall prosper in the land of promise" (1 Nephi 4:14). In contemplating the Lord's command to Nephi to kill Laban, this promise became part of Nephi's justification for the deed. This statement of prosperity based on obedience was repeated over and over to the Nephites in the coming centuries as a reminder to them of the blessings that would be theirs if they were faithful in living the gospel in their new homeland (1 Nephi 17:13–15; Omni 1:6; Mosiah 2:22).

Lehi reflected on the covenant between himself and Deity: "And he hath said that: Inasmuch as ye shall keep my commandments ye shall prosper in the land; but inasmuch as ye will not keep my commandments ye shall be cut off from my presence" (2 Nephi 1:20). Here we have both the positive and the negative aspects of the covenant—Plan A and Plan B, as I have designated them. Plan A leads to joy and prosperity, while Plan B leads to the divine broom sweeping the inhabitants from the land. Lehi detailed some additional elements of the covenant:

> Wherefore, this land is consecrated unto him whom he shall bring. And if it so be that they shall serve him according to the

commandments which he hath given, it shall be a land of liberty unto them; wherefore, they shall never be brought down into captivity; . . .

Wherefore, I, Lehi, have obtained a promise, that inasmuch as those whom the Lord God shall bring out of the land of Jerusalem shall keep his commandments, they shall prosper upon the face of this land; and they shall be kept from all other nations, that they may possess this land unto themselves.

And if it so be that they shall keep his commandments they shall be blessed upon the face of this land, and there shall be none to molest them, nor to take away the land of their inheritance; and they shall dwell safely forever." (2 Nephi 1:7–9)

The accompanying chart summarizes the covenant.

GOD PROMISES THE INHABITANTS	THE INHABITANTS COVENANT
1. They may possess this land of promise.	1. They must serve the God of the land—Jesus Christ.
2. They will be free from bondage.	2. They must keep God's commandments.
3. They will prosper in the land.	3. They must repent of their sins.
4. They will have sole possession of the land.	
5. The will dwell safely on the land forever.	
6. They will be kept from the knowledge of other nations who might overrun them if they knew of them.	

These promises and blessings were passed on to succeeding generations. Enos, for example, was concerned about the spiritual conditions of the Lamanites. The Lord told him, "I will visit thy brethren according to their diligence in keeping my commandments. I have given unto them this land, and it is a holy land; and I curse it not save it be for the cause of iniquity" (Enos 1:10). Jarom, Enos's son who lived some two hundred years after Lehi, speaking from hindsight and from his own experience, said, "The word of the Lord was verified, which he spake unto our fathers, saying that: Inasmuch as ye will keep my commandments ye shall prosper in the land" (Jarom 1:9). Omni gave this witness: "For the Lord would not suffer, after he had led them out of the land of Jerusalem and kept and preserved them from falling into the hands of their enemies, yea, he would not suffer that the words should not be verified, which he spake unto our father, saying that: Inasmuch as ye will not keep my commandments ye shall not prosper in the land" (Omni 1:6).

The knowledge of this covenant between God and the land's inhabitants continued in the large plates of Nephi and it was repeated by a number of prophets through the remainder of the Nephite history. The Savior, in His visit to the Nephites, also reminded them of the promises upon the land in the last days.[2]

Stage 3: God Establishes Laws for the Governance of the People

The Nephites came to this land from the tradition and background of the law of Moses. The law was written on the brass plates, and Nephi knew that his people needed the law if they were to survive in their new land: "I also thought that they could not keep the commandments of the Lord according to the law of Moses, save they should have the law. And I also knew that the law was engraven upon the plates of brass" (1 Nephi 4:15–16). After the sons of Lehi obtained the plates, Lehi perused them and "beheld that they did contain the five books of Moses" (1 Nephi 5:11). The law of God was written on that portion of the ancient record.

In a later sermon, Nephi said, "Notwithstanding we believe in

Christ, we keep the law of Moses, and look forward with steadfastness unto Christ, until the law shall be fulfilled" (2 Nephi 25:24). There are a number of references throughout the Book of Mormon that relate to the law of Moses. When King Mosiah came to the throne, however, it is reasonable to assume that in altering the form of government from kings to judges, additional laws or amendments would be necessary to suit the changed situation of the Nephites. Normally, when people are righteous, laws such as the Ten Commandments are easily embraced. However, the more wicked people become, the more detailed laws must be.

Stage 4: When Most of the People Choose Evil over Good, the Covenant Is Breached

When Mosiah's sons chose missionary work over kingship, the form of government was changed and the ruler described how such a system should work. It involved higher and lower judges that would be elected by the people, a bold experiment in self-government after a long period of being ruled by kings. It also speaks highly of King Mosiah, who, like his father Benjamin, was not grasping for power, but was more interested in the spiritual development of his people. He gave this counsel to the people in forming a new government: "Therefore, choose you by the voice of this people judges, that ye may be judged according to *the laws which have been given you by our fathers, which are correct, and which were given them by the hand of the Lord*" (Mosiah 29:25; italics added). The laws under which the Nephites lived were, like the constitutional law of the Gentiles upon this land in our day, inspired from heaven.

The wise king noted: "Now it is not common that the voice of the people desireth anything contrary to that which is right; but *it is common for the lesser part of the people to desire that which is not right;*

therefore this shall ye observe and make it your law—to *do your business by the voice of the people*" (Mosiah 29: 26; italics added). This counsel is relevant to our present political system. When people are righteous and the laws are fairly and impartially administered, people are easy to govern. If they are not, there will always be a minority pushing a more extreme agenda on both ends of the political spectrum. In American politics we think in terms of "liberals" who want more government influence and control, and "conservatives," who generally want less governmental interference. The *extremes* of both positions are unhealthy. Stay away from the fringes, the king counseled. Stay in the mainstream. Don't stray from the will of the righteous majority.

Nonetheless, King Mosiah pointed out the danger of self-government: "If the time comes that the voice of the people doth choose iniquity, then is the time that the judgments of God will come upon you; yea, *then is the time he will visit you with great destruction even as he has hitherto visited this land*" (Mosiah 29:27; italics added).

When the majority of the people gravitate toward wickedness, they agitate to change the laws lest the laws condemn them and their behavior. However, because the laws of the Nephites came from a divine source, the laws are not to be changed to support or sustain wickedness. Because fair laws, strictly enforced, are not kind to the wicked, the wicked want to amend the laws sustained by the majority in order to support their own selfish or greedy causes. Justice requires punishment when the law is broken, or invokes severe sanctions on the offenders. Wicked people like a liberal interpretation of the law; otherwise they will be punished by the law's provisions. They could be imprisoned. They argue that their freedom is restricted. They reason that their offenses are too harsh. Korihor took advantage of this system by using freedom of speech to contend against the Church, because "there was no law against a man's belief; for it was strictly contrary to the commands of God that there should be a law which should bring men on to unequal grounds. . . . There was no law against a man's belief; therefore, a man was punished only for the crimes which he had done" (Alma 30: 7–11).

The Book of Mormon prophets were firm in their counsel that strongly enforced fair and equitable laws, as determined by the people, administered without regard to race, income, or socio-economic status, greatly benefit society. Mercy, of course, comes into play when genuine repentance and restitution is offered. Penalties associated with breaking laws should be explicit and well-publicized so that all are aware of the consequences of their actions.

The Nephites established a tier of judges that included provisions for dealing with a variety of crimes. An appeal of the judges' verdict was possible, something unheard of in a kingship form of government. "And it came to pass that they did appoint judges to rule over them, or to judge them according to the law; and this they did throughout all the land" (Mosiah 29:41). "And now if ye have judges, and they do not judge you according to the law which has been given, ye can cause that they may be judged of a higher judge" (Mosiah 29:28). Alma was appointed to be the first chief judge (Mosiah 29:42).

Despite good laws, the Nephites remind us of a yo-yo. They were righteous for a time. Then pride and arrogance consumed them, and they went through a period of selfishness that led to extreme wickedness on their part. Moreover, the Nephites had an enemy who were dedicated to their destruction. The Lamanites, Nephi was told very early by the Lord, would be a constant thorn in the side of the Nephites if they turned to wickedness:

"Inasmuch as thy brethren shall rebel against thee, they shall be cut off from the presence of the Lord. And inasmuch as thou shalt keep my commandments, thou shalt be made a ruler and a teacher over thy brethren" (1 Nephi 2:21–22).

Thus, Nephi and his followers were favored over the Lamanites only because of their righteousness. Then the Lord bluntly gave Nephi this warning: "For behold, in that day that they shall rebel against me, I will curse them even with a sore curse, and they shall have no power over thy seed except they shall rebel against me also. And if it so be that they [the Nephites] rebel against me, they [the Lamanites] shall be a *scourge unto thy seed, to stir them up in the ways of remembrance*" (1 Nephi 2:23–24; italics added). That one sentence encapsulates the entire story of the book! Whenever the Nephites were careless in living their covenants, the Lamanites took up arms against them and humbled them.

Jacob confirmed the principle. To his fellow Nephites, he said: "For except ye repent the land is cursed for your sakes; and the Lamanites, which are not filthy like unto you, . . . shall scourge you even unto destruction. And the time speedily cometh, that except ye repent they shall possess the land of your inheritance, and the Lord God will lead away the righteous out from among you" (Jacob 3:3–4).

As we examine the Nephite story in more detail, we find that the majority of people did, in fact, begin to choose evil over good. Within ten years of the time that King Mosiah explained the principle of self-government to the people, the majority began to make evil choices. Iniquity always seems to develop in an environment where the legal system is subverted. Mormon, the primary abridger, explained the problem: "Now it was those men who sought to destroy them, who were lawyers, who were hired or appointed by the people to administer the law at their times of trials, or at the trials of the crimes of the people before the judges. Now these lawyers were learned in all the arts and cunning of the people; and this was to enable them that they might be skilful in their profession" (Alma 10:14–15).

These verses suggest that one of the functions of defense attorneys is to find ways to free the guilty, particularly if the guilty have enough money or friends in high places to hire the most "skilful" lawyers. Amulek, upon witnessing the arguments of the lawyers attempting to destroy Alma and himself, observed: "And now behold, I say unto you that *the foundation of the destruction of this people is beginning to be laid by the unrighteousness of your lawyers and your judges* (Alma 10:27; italics added).

When the integrity of lawyers and judges is compromised, the judicial system is no longer a blessing to the people. This becomes a more serious problem when we remember that the laws in place to regulate rules of conduct originated not with man but with a higher Source (Helaman 4:22). Divine laws cannot be changed, modified, watered down, or ignored without serious repercussions, both physical and spiritual. The verbal exchanges between the prophets and the lawyers in the scriptural record are indicative of the age-old problem of the wicked trying to justify their wickedness. The Savior faced the same problem with the scribes and religionists of His day, and it led to His persecution and trial (2 Nephi 10:5–6). If the legal system can be corrupted, then justice and mercy cannot operate fairly in behalf of the citizens. When that occurs, too often the innocent suffer while the guilty go free.

When we follow the Nephites for fifty or sixty years after Mosiah's counsel, we see the wisdom of the king's words. The record says, "For as their laws and their governments were established by the voice of the people, and *they who chose evil were more numerous than they who chose good, therefore they were ripening for destruction,* for the laws had become corrupted. Yea, and this was not all; they were a stiffnecked people, insomuch that they could not be governed by the law nor justice, save it were to their destruction" (Helaman 5:2–3; italics added).

Suppose, for example, there is a law that states that adultery is punishable by fine or imprisonment or both (the law of Moses imposed death). When people are righteous, the law will be infrequently exercised because good people refrain from adulterous behavior. If, however, the majority begins to argue that there are times when such actions might be justified, then adultery increases and strict enforcement of the law would require society to build more places of incarceration, or government revenue would rise, or both. When society begins to believe that there is no harm in adultery, the law is ignored. But the problem in this promised land is that we cannot ignore laws concerning adultery because the law against it is one of the Ten Commandments. God does not wink at adultery. He "cannot look upon sin with the least degree of allowance" (D&C 1:31). *Therefore, in letting adultery go unpunished, people violate an important element of the covenant that exists on the land.*

His experience in seeing the legal system being compromised to excuse sinful behavior caused Mormon to reflect on the condition of the people. After a few battles, he observed of the Nephites:

> Yea, they began to remember the prophecies of Alma, and also the words of Mosiah; and they saw that they had been a stiffnecked people, and that they had set at naught the commandments of God;
>
> And that *they had altered and trampled under their feet the laws of Mosiah,* or *that which the Lord commanded him to give unto the people;* and *they saw that their laws had become corrupted, and that they had become a wicked people,* inasmuch that they were wicked even like unto the Lamanites. . . .
>
> Therefore *the Lord did cease to preserve them by his miraculous and matchless power,* for they had fallen into a state of unbelief and awful wickedness." (Helaman 4:21–25; italics added)

Stage 5: The Lord Warns the Inhabitants When They Are in Danger of Being Swept Off

Before judgments are meted out to those "ripening" in wickedness, the Lord sends prophets and missionaries out to warn the people of the need to repent. Much of the Bible and Book of Mormon narrative records the message of prophets sent to call people to repentance. That situation unfolded at least six times with the Jaredites. Calling the people to repentance is one of the principal roles of prophets when the people are evil. They monitor the righteousness of society at large and then encourage or caution people about what needs to be changed, started, stopped, emphasized, or implemented. Sometimes prophets compliment people on their choices. We understand this principle as we listen to general conferences of the Church. At times, the Brethren warn us of dangers within our society (movies, videos, Internet misuse, pornography, divorce, abuse, and so forth) or practices offensive to God (Sabbath violation, temper, dishonesty, spouse abuse, laziness, and so on). The messages of the prophets vary according to the diligence of the people. Jacob's denunciation of his people, for example, contrasts with the encouragement King Benjamin gave his people, who were humbled by his message and desired to live righteously (Jacob 2; Mosiah 5).

Stage 6: The Inhabitants Respond to the Warnings from God's Servants

When prophets deliver messages of reproof, people generally respond in one of three ways: they accept the message, repent, and join the Church (or become active again); they reject (in varying degrees) the message and the messenger; they tolerate those they may view as a nuisance, but because the law of the land allows freedom of religion, they simply ignore the message and close their door. Missionaries are familiar with these three responses.

When people accept the message and join the Church or become active once again, they revert to Stages 2 and 3, in which laws, commandments, and covenants are again understood. When people simply tolerate the message of the missionaries, some will be converted, depending on the level of righteousness or wickedness among the people and the attitude of the government in sustaining or impinging on the principle of freedom of religion. These factors play an important role in the progress of our current missionary efforts throughout the world. When the message is rejected, the people move to Stage 7.

Stage 7: When the People Reject Prophetic Warnings, the Judgments of God Begin

As people reject the counsel of prophets and missionaries, the judgments of God commence as a warning to the people that they are making choices contrary to God's commandments and that they are violating the covenant on the land. Judgments may include famine (2 Nephi 1:18; 6:15; Alma 10:22), pestilence (disease) (Mosiah 12:4; Alma 45:11), or the sword (war) (Alma 62:39; Helaman 13:9). Drought or floods come naturally as a part of the weather patterns, of course, but they may also be a part of divine judgments. For example, on this land of promise, not many years before the Savior's birth, the following events took place:

> There arose a great storm, such an one as never had been known in all the land.
>
> And there was also a great and terrible tempest; and there was terrible thunder, insomuch that it did shake the whole earth as if it was about to divide asunder.
>
> And there were exceedingly sharp lightnings, such as never had been known in all the land. (3 Nephi 8:5–7)

With economic prosperity, people seem to divide themselves into social, financial, and educational strata. Such inequalities are never positive factors in the social order. The "haves" begin to persecute the "have-nots" and vice versa. The "have-nots" covet what the more wealthy members of society possess, and the "haves" never believe they have enough. People are likely to forget their common heritage as children of God, and they often revert to selfishness and prideful behavior. Perhaps the best sermon on this problem was given by Mormon as he summarized the words of Nephi, the son of Helaman:

> Yea, and we may see at the very time when he doth prosper his people, yea, in the increase of their fields, their flocks and their herds, and in gold, and in silver, and in all manner of precious things of every kind and art; sparing their lives, and delivering them out of the hands of their enemies; softening the hearts of their enemies that they should not declare wars against them; yea, and in fine, doing all things for the welfare and happiness of his people; yea, then is the time that they do harden their hearts, and do forget the Lord their God, and do trample under their feet the Holy One—yea, and this because of their ease, and their exceedingly great prosperity.
>
> And thus we see that except the Lord doth chasten his people with many afflictions, yea, except he doth visit them with death and with terror, and with famine and with all manner of pestilence, they will not remember him. (Helaman 12:2–3)

Pride was a major stumbling block to the Nephites, and its seeds germinated in the fields of prosperity and material gain: "And it came to pass that the fifty and second year ended in peace also, save it were the exceedingly great pride which had gotten into the hearts of the people; and it was because of their exceedingly great riches and their prosperity in the land; and it did grow upon them from day to day" (Helaman 3:36).

Stage 8: The Spirit of the Lord
Withdraws from the People

When people transgress the laws of God, when they refuse to listen to their prophets, when they ignore the laws set up by the hand of God, when they violate covenants with Deity with impunity, they lose the Spirit of the Lord and revert to what King Benjamin called the "natural man." He described the "natural man" as one who

> is an enemy to God, and has been from the fall of Adam, and will be, forever and ever, unless he yields to the enticings of the Holy Spirit, and putteth off the natural man and becometh a saint through the atonement of Christ the Lord, and becometh as a child, submissive, meek, humble, patient, full of love, willing to submit to all things which the Lord seeth fit to inflict upon him, even as a child doth submit to his father. (Mosiah 3:19)

We see the natural consequences of a loss of the Spirit among the Nephites as they grew in wickedness: "And thus we see that the Nephites did begin to dwindle in unbelief, and grow in wickedness and abominations. . . . And thus we see that the Spirit of the Lord began to withdraw from the Nephites, because of the wickedness and the hardness of their hearts" (Helaman 6:34–35).

The Lord warned, "Because of the hardness of the hearts of the people of the Nephites, except they repent I will take away my word from them, and I will withdraw my Spirit from them, and I will suffer them no longer, and I will turn the hearts of their brethren against them" (Helaman 13:8). The Lord will not tolerate wickedness without a withdrawal of His Spirit.

When people lose the desire to live righteously, to please God, to bless each other, when they sin against that light given to all men who come into the world, then society quickly crumbles. When laws are ignored routinely, integrity suffers, lawlessness abounds, commerce is interrupted, society disintegrates into chaos, and men move selfishly to protect their few possessions. Their destruction is not far behind.

Stage 9: The Inhabitants Become Fully Ripened in Iniquity and Cast Out the Righteous

As people ripen in iniquity, they don't want anyone, especially the righteous, to remind them of their evil ways. Such a message is irritating and depressing and pricks at their consciences. They desire to cast out the "religious right" or to destroy those crying repentance to them. When people no longer will listen to those whose sole effort is directed to save them from possible catastrophes, they are ripened to the point where they are good for nothing except to be cast out or destroyed. Two scriptures describe this process among the Nephites:

> Yea, and I say unto you that if it were not for the prayers of the righteous, who are now in the land, that ye would even now be visited with utter destruction; yet it would not be by flood, as were the people in the days of Noah, but it would be by famine, and by pestilence, and the sword.
>
> But it is by the prayers of the righteous that ye are spared; now therefore, if ye will cast out the righteous from among you then will not the Lord stay his hand; but in his fierce anger he will come out against you; then ye shall be smitten by famine, and by pestilence, and by the sword; and the time is soon at hand except ye repent. (Alma 10:22–23)

And from a later sermon,

> Yea, wo unto this great city of Zarahemla; for behold it is because of those who are righteous that it is saved; yea, wo unto

THE RISE AND FALL OF THE NEPHITES AND MULEKITES

this great city, for I perceive, saith the Lord, that there are many, yea, even the more part of this great city, that will harden their hearts against me, saith the Lord.

But blessed are they who will repent, for them will I spare. But behold, if it were not for the righteous who are in this great city, behold, I would cause that fire should come down out of heaven and destroy it.

But behold, it is for the righteous' sake that it is spared. But behold, the time cometh, saith the Lord, that when ye shall cast out the righteous from among you, then shall ye be ripe for destruction; yea, wo be unto this great city, because of the wickedness and abominations which are in her. (Helaman 13:12–14)

Ripening is a word used in the scriptures to describe the deepening of wickedness that comes when a people moves from righteousness to evil.[3] When people become fully ripe in iniquity, unless they sincerely and immediately repent, they are destroyed.

Stage 10: The Wicked Are Destroyed

The first civilizations on this land were destroyed by flood and civil war. The Nephites had two options open to them: repent, or continue to choose evil and suffer the consequences. Both Lehi and Nephi saw in vision the future destruction of their people many centuries before it actually took place, and they wept over the decisions of Laman and Lemuel. Lehi saw that his children would be divided and that the Nephites, despite prophets, scriptures, and revelation, would be decimated by the Lamanites because of their turning away from the God of heaven, even though the Son of God would later minister unto them. They also saw that the Lamanites would be smitten by the hand of the later Gentile inhabitants. He lamented:

But behold, when the time cometh that they shall dwindle in unbelief, after they have received so great blessings from the hand of the Lord . . . behold, I say, if the day shall come that they will reject the Holy One of Israel, the true Messiah, their Redeemer and their God, behold, the judgments of him that is just shall rest upon them.

Yea, he will bring other nations unto them, and he will give unto them power, and he will take away from them the lands of their possessions, and he will cause them to be scattered and smitten. (2 Nephi 1:10–11)

Father Lehi further warned Laman and Lemuel that they would be "cut off and destroyed forever; or, that a cursing should come upon you for the space of many generations; and ye are visited by sword, and by famine, and are hated, and are led according to the will and captivity of the devil" (2 Nephi 1:17–18). Already knowing the outcome, however, he said, "But behold, his will be done; for his ways are righteousness forever" (2 Nephi 1:19). Lehi reviewed the covenant with his family so they would not mistake the divine rule: "Inasmuch as ye shall keep my commandments ye shall prosper in the land; but inasmuch as ye will not keep my commandments ye shall be cut off from my presence" (2 Nephi 1:20).

Of course, the Nephites were not destroyed for many centuries after Lehi's death. But as their wickedness increased in the days of Mormon and Moroni, the dire predictions began to be fulfilled:

But, behold, I say unto you that if ye persist in your wickedness that your days shall not be prolonged in the land, for the Lamanites shall be sent upon you; and if ye repent not they shall come in a time when you know not, and ye shall be visited with utter destruction; and it shall be according to the fierce anger of the Lord.

For he will not suffer you that ye shall live in your iniquities, to destroy his people. I say unto you, Nay; he would rather suffer that the Lamanites might destroy all his people who are called the people of Nephi, if it were possible that they could fall into sins and transgressions, after having had so much light and so much knowledge given unto them of the Lord their God;

Yea, after having been such a highly favored people of the Lord; yea, after having been favored above every other nation, kindred, tongue, or people; after having had all things made known unto them, according to their desires, and their faith, and prayers, of that which has been, and which is, and which is to come. (Alma 9:18–20)

In fact, these conditions fit the days of Mormon or Moroni as well as Alma. Moroni described the conditions that prevailed in his own day:

And now it came to pass that after the great and tremendous battle at Cumorah, behold, the Nephites who had escaped into the country southward were hunted by the Lamanites, until they were all destroyed. And my father also was killed by them, and I even remain alone to write the sad tale of the destruction of my people. But behold, they are gone, and I fulfil the commandment of my father. (Mormon 8:2–3)

Moroni summarized the extent of death and destruction that came upon the Nephites and explained its origin:

And behold, the Lamanites have hunted my people, the Nephites, down from city to city and from place to place, even until they are no more; and great has been their fall; yea, great and marvelous is the destruction of my people, the Nephites. And behold, *it is the hand of the Lord which hath done it.* (Mormon 8:7–8; italics added)

139

Thus Mormon's earlier declaration about the destruction of his people and the apostasy of the Lamanites was confirmed:

> They were once a delightsome people, and they had Christ for their shepherd; yea, they were led even by God the Father.
> But now, behold, they are led about by Satan. . . .
> And behold, the Lord hath reserved their blessings, which they might have received in the land, for the Gentiles who shall possess the land.
> But behold, it shall come to pass that they shall be driven and scattered by the Gentiles. (Mormon 5:17–20)

Sadly, we come to the end of the great Nephite nation. It was a terrible finale after all the Nephites had known and experienced, including a visit from the Savior Himself when He had taught them the gospel. Even Mormon was killed. Only Moroni was preserved to ensure that the record would come forth in the latter days unto the Gentiles. Why the Lamanites were not destroyed is worth our examination.

11

The Survival of
the Lamanites

The initial Lamanites descended from Laman and Lemuel, the two oldest sons of Lehi and Sariah.[1] The rebellion of these two sons against their father Lehi and their brother Nephi began soon after the family departed from Jerusalem on the way to the land of promise. Nephi indicated that his brothers wished to return to Jerusalem. Lehi made a conscientious effort to help these two sons understand the importance of their journey. When they arrived at the first stopping place in the wilderness, for example, Lehi named the nearby river after Laman and the valley after Lemuel. No doubt Lehi was trying to encourage these two sons to change their attitude, become an integral part of the family, be cheerful about the journey they were undertaking. Nephi stated that Lehi did this "because of the stiff-neckedness of Laman and Lemuel; for behold they did murmur in many things against their father" (1 Nephi 2:11). The first chapters of the Book of Mormon contain a litany of murmurings by Laman and Lemuel against parent and brother. It greatly saddened Nephi that "Laman and Lemuel would not hearken unto my words; and being grieved because of the hardness of their hearts I cried unto the Lord for them" (1 Nephi 2:18).[2]

The history of the Lehites is practically one long battle between the opposing Nephite and Lamanite factions. The spiritual damage caused by these two older brothers over the course of the history of the Nephite civilization is incalculable and serves as a witness as to the long-term effect that a rebellious family member has over his own posterity and others over a period of many generations. Enos, for example, in his prayer in behalf of the Lamanites, said, "Wherefore, I did pour out my whole soul unto God for them. . . . For at the present our strugglings were vain in restoring them to the true faith. And they swore in their wrath that, if it were possible, they would destroy our records and us, and also all the traditions of our fathers" (Enos 1:9–14).

Father Lehi knew from his dream concerning the tree of life (1 Nephi 8) that his two oldest sons would not remain faithful nor choose righteousness in the long run, yet he repeatedly tried to teach and warn them of the dangers they would face if they continued in their rebellion. But, he was unable, even in his last sermon to them, to turn them from their chosen course. They continued the persecution of Nephi until finally the Nephites were forced to separate from their brothers to a land named after Nephi. Much of Lehi's last counsel to his posterity was a chastisement of his wayward sons. He pleaded with them to follow their younger brother: "Rebel no more against your brother, whose views have been glorious," but his plea was in vain (2 Nephi 1:24).

Lehi taught the family the overall principle: "Inasmuch as ye shall keep my commandments ye shall prosper in the land; and inasmuch as ye will not keep my commandments ye shall be cut off from my presence" (2 Nephi 4:4). Then, in an effort to negate or minimize the effect of waywardness of the two oldest sons on their posterity, Lehi blessed Laman's children that they would not be swept off the land:

But behold, my sons and my daughters, I cannot go down to my grave save I should leave a blessing upon you; for behold, I know that if ye are brought up in the way ye should go ye will not depart from it.

Wherefore, if ye are cursed, behold, I leave my blessing upon you, *that the cursing may be taken from you* and be answered upon the heads of your parents.

Wherefore, *because of my blessing the Lord God will not suffer that ye shall perish;* wherefore, he will be merciful unto you and unto your seed *forever.* (2 Nephi 4:5–7; italics added)

To the children of Lemuel, Lehi gave a similar promise:

Behold, my sons and my daughters, who are the sons and the daughters of my second son; behold I leave unto you the same blessing which I left unto the sons and daughters of Laman; wherefore, *thou shalt not utterly be destroyed; but in the end they seed shall be blessed.* (2 Nephi 4:9; italics added)

Today we are see large numbers of Lamanites coming into the Church, particularly in Mexico and in Central and South America. It appears that the blessings Lehi left upon his grandchildren are being realized today. One profound instance of the latter-day fulfillment of prophecy to Lehi's seed by a member of the Quorum of Twelve Apostles came through Elder Melvin J. Ballard when he dedicated South America for the preaching of the gospel. Elder Melvin J. Ballard's grandson M. Russell Ballard, also a member of the Quorum of the Twelve, stated:

On 4 July 1926, Grandfather said:
"The work of the Lord will grow slowly for a time here just as an oak grows slowly from an acorn. It will not shoot up in a day as does the sunflower that grows quickly and then dies. But thousands will join the Church here. It will be divided into

more than one mission and will be one of the strongest in the Church. The work here is the smallest that it will ever be. *The day will come when the Lamanites in this land will be given a chance. The South American Mission will be a power in the Church.*" (Vernon Sharp diary, in Melvin J. Ballard, [*Crusader for Righteousness*], p. 84). (Ballard, "Kingdom Rolls Forth in South America," 13; italics added)

How profoundly the Church has been affected by the growth of Church membership among the Lamanites. Elder H. Verlan Andersen observed concerning the work among the Lamanites in South America:

> During the past few years, my wife and I have served as missionaries in Latin American countries. . . . It has been deeply satisfying to work with those lovable and believing people and to see the prophecies of the Book of Mormon being fulfilled as hundreds of thousands of the descendants of Lehi join the Church. The day of the Lamanites has truly arrived.
>
> The history of the Lamanites just before the Lord's first appearance on this continent reveals an interesting parallel between what occurred then and what is happening today. Commencing about the year 92 B.C., the Lamanites began coming into the Lord's Church by the tens of thousands. That conversion miracle, which took place just shortly before the Lord's first advent, is being repeated now just prior to his second coming. ("Missionary Work Is the Lifeblood of the Church," 23)

Preserving the Lamanites in the Land

There were times in the Book of Mormon account when the Lamanites were more righteous than the Nephites. "Ye have done greater iniquities than the Lamanites, our brethren," Jacob chastised his people (Jacob 2:35). "Behold, the Lamanites your brethren, whom ye hate because of their filthiness and the cursing which hath come upon their skins, *are more righteous than you*" (Jacob 3:5; italics added). Then he predicted that the Lamanites would be preserved in the land: "Wherefore, because of this observance, in keeping this commandment, the Lord God will not destroy them, but will be merciful unto them; and one day they shall become a blessed people" (Jacob 3:6).

Then, in a particularly severe rebuke, Jacob compared the behavior of the Nephite men to that of the Lamanite men: "Behold, their husbands love their wives, and their wives love their husbands; and their husbands and their wives love their children; and their unbelief and their hatred towards you is because of the iniquity of their fathers; wherefore, how much better are you than they, in the sight of your great Creator?" (Jacob 3:7). Jacob's rebuke came hundreds of years before the Savior visited the Nephites.

During the mission of Alma and Amulek to the people of Ammonihah, Alma rebuked the wicked of that city, saying, "it would be far more tolerable for the Lamanites than for them" in the day of judgment. For, he said, "The promises of the Lord are extended to the Lamanites, but they are not unto you if ye transgress" (Alma 9:23–24).

A few decades before the appearance of the resurrected Lord at Bountiful, Nephi, the son of Helaman, explained the consequences of the Nephites' wickedness in contrast to the Lamanites:

> I would that ye should behold, my brethren, that it shall be better for the Lamanites than for you except ye shall repent.
>
> For behold, they are more righteous than you, for they have not sinned against that great knowledge which ye have received; therefore the Lord will be merciful unto them; yea, he will lengthen out their days and increase their seed, even when thou

shalt be utterly destroyed except thou shalt repent. (Helaman 7:23–24)

Nephi revealed the source of this inspired insight:

> I do not say that these things shall be, of myself, because it is not of myself that I know these things; but behold, I know that these things are true because the Lord God has made them known unto me. (Helaman 7:29)

It appears that the Lamanites were not destroyed, in part because they did not have access to scriptural records throughout most of their history and in part because they had few prophets among them. Thus, they were not as spiritually accountable as were the Nephites who had both the written record and living oracles. Nephi explained that the promises of the Lord were extended to the Lamanites because had the Lamanites had the gospel rather than the Nephites the outcome would have been different:

> And now, because of their steadfastness when they do believe in that thing which they do believe, for because of their firmness when they are once-enlightened, behold, the Lord shall bless them and prolong their days, notwithstanding their iniquity—
>
> Yea, even if they should dwindle in unbelief the Lord shall prolong their days, until the time shall come which hath been spoken of by our fathers, and also by the prophet Zenos, and many other prophets, concerning the restoration of our brethren, the Lamanites, again to the knowledge of the truth—
>
> Yea, I say unto you, that in the latter times the promises of the Lord have been extended to our brethren, the Lamanites; and notwithstanding the many afflictions which they shall have, and notwithstanding they shall be driven to and fro upon the face of the earth, and be hunted, and shall be smitten and

scattered abroad, having no place for refuge, the Lord shall be merciful unto them.

And this is according to the prophecy, that they shall again be brought to the true knowledge, which is the knowledge of their Redeemer, and their great and true shepherd, and be numbered among his sheep.

Therefore I say unto you, it shall be better for them than for you except ye repent.

For behold, had the mighty works been shown unto them which have been shown unto you, yea, unto them who have dwindled in unbelief because of the traditions of their fathers, ye can see of yourselves that they never would again have dwindled in unbelief.

Therefore, saith the Lord: I will not utterly destroy them, but I will cause that in the day of my wisdom they shall return again unto me, saith the Lord.

And now behold, saith the Lord, concerning the people of the Nephites: If they will not repent, and observe to do my will, *I will utterly destroy them,* saith the Lord, *because of their unbelief notwithstanding the many mighty works which I have done among them;* and as surely as the Lord liveth shall these things be, saith the Lord. (Helaman 15:10–17; italics added)

The Lamanites Were Preserved

There are several reasons why the Lamanites were preserved in the land. First, Lehi and later prophets prayed mightily to God to preserve them. They asked the Lord to preserve a record so that at some future day the Lamanites would learn the gospel. These servants of the Lord asked Him to turn their hearts to the gospel in their day as well as in the latter days. Second, the Lamanites, during several periods of history were more righteous than the Nephites

(Helaman 6:1, 34, 36; 13:10). The Nephites had possession of the scriptures and were blessed of the Lord initially, but eventually they apostatized from the truth and ripened to such a state of iniquity that the Lord used the Lamanites to sweep the Nephites from the land, as He had indicated to Nephi that He would (1 Nephi 2:21–24).

Unfortunately, after they swept the Nephites from the land, the Lamanites remained in a state of apostasy and became more primitive for centuries without the gospel or the priesthood in their lives. "The Lamanites are at war one with another," Moroni explained, "and the whole face of this land is one continual round of murder and bloodshed; and no one knoweth the end of the war. And there are none save it be the Lamanites and robbers that do exist upon the face of the land" (Mormon 8:8–9). When the destruction of the Nephites was complete, the Lamanites remained scattered, which was their condition when Columbus found them. From that point on, the Lamanites suffered great destruction at the hands of the advancing Gentile civilization in both North and South America. Native Americans in the United States were killed outright, moved off lands, placed on reservations, and treated shabbily by the incoming settlers, just as Lehi had predicted (2 Nephi 1:11). This outcome was foreseen by ancient prophets—Isaiah (29:1–4) as well as Lehi, Nephi, and their successors upon this continent.

Mormon lamented the great loss and the fate of the Lamanites:

> But now, behold, they are led about by Satan. . . .
>
> And behold, the Lord hath reserved their blessings, which they might have received in the land, for the Gentiles who shall possess the land.
>
> But behold, it shall come to pass that they shall be driven and scattered by the Gentiles; and after they have been driven and scattered by the Gentiles, behold, then will the Lord remember the covenant which he made unto Abraham and unto all the house of Israel. (Mormon 5:18–20)

The Arrival of the Gentiles

Nephi foresaw the Gentiles come upon the land and destroy many Lamanites, but the Lord promised Nephi that his brothers' posterity would not be annihilated: "Thou seest that the Lord God will not suffer that the Gentiles will utterly destroy the mixture of thy seed, which are among thy brethren. Neither will he suffer that the Gentiles shall destroy the seed of thy brethren" (1 Nephi 13:30–31).

Perhaps because the Lamanites were scattered over the two continents, the Lord used the Gentiles to prepare this land for the final dispensation of the gospel and the priesthood to the earth before the reign of Jesus Christ and the coming of the New Jerusalem (Ether 13:3–4, 10). That nation has now been established, and the land has been greatly blessed in consequence of the restoration of the Church and kingdom of God on the earth (3 Nephi 21:4–6). The form of government established by the Gentiles, a constitutional form rather than a monarchy, allows freedom and liberty to all, as Jacob foresaw: "But behold, this land, said God . . . shall be a land of liberty unto the Gentiles, and there shall be no kings upon the land, who shall raise up unto the Gentiles. And I will fortify this land against all other nations" (2 Nephi 10:10–12).

Thus the Nephites were destroyed in a civil war, yet the Lamanites were without God and Christ in the land, and the times of the Gentiles began (D&C 45:28) with the arrival of Columbus and other Christians from Europe and Great Britain (1 Nephi 13:12–13). The Book of Mormon was preserved and restored for our day to provide an account of what happened to these earlier inhabitants. Mormon wrote on the first page of his record: "Written to the Lamanites, who are a remnant of the house of Israel; and also to Jew and Gentile" (Book of Mormon title page). Truly, the book was preserved for a day when the seed of Lehi would have access to the sacred records of their progenitors, and unlike Laman and Lemuel, these latter-day citizens "shall blossom as the rose" before the coming of the Lord (D&C 49:24).

Today we are witnessing a great gathering of Lamanites as they come into the Church in large numbers. The areas of fastest growth in Church membership are in the lands of the Lamanites south of the United States. Surely, Lehi's promise to his posterity is finally in the process of being fulfilled.

12

The Fate of the Gentiles

We have traced the Antediluvians, the Jaredites, the Mulekites, and the Nephites through their rise to greatness as a people, only to see them fall into patterns of wickedness that led to their downfall. We will now consider the fate of the Gentiles, the present occupants of the land. What happens to them is important to Latter-day Saints, for we live in the midst of their culture. We are a part of them. In the Prophet Joseph Smith's prayer at the dedication of the Kirtland Temple, he prayed, "Now these words, O Lord, we have spoken before thee, concerning the revelations and commandments which thou hast given unto us, who are *identified with the Gentiles*" (D&C 109:60; italics added). The title page of the Book of Mormon indicates that the book is written for the benefit of the Gentiles also. The Lord allowed the Gentiles to establish a great political and economic system to *bless the house of Israel* in the latter days, to bring the gospel to the remnants of Israel (1 Nephi 15:13–14). Because the gospel and the priesthood were restored to the Gentiles on this land, Latter-day Saints have the responsibility to share the message of the

Restoration with those Gentiles who do not believe in Jesus Christ (3 Nephi 16:8).

Stage 1: The Lord Leads the Righteous to a Promised Land

Nephi beheld in vision the coming of the Gentiles to the promised land:

> And I looked and beheld a man among the Gentiles, who was separated from the seed of my brethren by the many waters; and I beheld the Spirit of God, that it came down and wrought upon the man; and he went forth upon the many waters, even unto the seed of my brethren, who were in the promised land.
>
> And it came to pass that I beheld the Spirit of God, that it wrought upon other Gentiles; and they went forth out of captivity, upon the many waters.
>
> And it came to pass that I beheld many multitudes of the Gentiles upon the land of promise." (1 Nephi 13:12–14)

Nephi described how the Lord assisted the Gentiles in gaining their independence from their "mother Gentiles." He saw the fledgling military of the Gentiles fight against those who "were gathered together upon the waters, and upon the land also, to battle against them." And he witnessed the miracle: "And I beheld that the power of God was with them, and also that the wrath of God was upon all those that were gathered together against them to battle. And I, Nephi, beheld that the Gentiles that had gone out of captivity were delivered by the power of God out of the hands of all other nations" (1 Nephi 13:17–19). The Lord assisted the colonists in their quest for freedom.

The Gentiles were given this land of promise because the

Nephites broke their covenants with Deity (Mormon 5:19). The clash between the Gentiles and the Lamanites, who had disintegrated into tribal factions, is a well-known part of American history. It was foretold by both Nephi and the Savior (1 Nephi 12; 13:31; 3 Nephi 16:8–9). The Lord promised Nephi, however, that He would not "suffer that the Gentiles shall destroy the seed of thy brethren" (1 Nephi 13:31).

Stage 2: God Covenants with the Inhabitants of the Land

The covenant on this land was not known to the Gentiles at the time they arrived. They knew that God had blessed them in obtaining this land as a place where freedom of religion and a political system was born, but not until the gospel was restored and the Book of Mormon published did it become evident that the Lord was involved in bringing them to this land and placing them under the same obligations to live righteously as the former inhabitants had been under. Perhaps for that reason, the Gentiles were (and still are) unaware of the covenant and therefore mercy has been extended to the Gentiles until Church members more fully present them the gospel. Our Father in Heaven has been patient with the immorality and wickedness that has taken place historically among the Gentiles and which is even now becoming more entrenched in the land. It is the role of Latter-day Saints to educate the Gentiles, if they will receive it, concerning the great promises extended to them by God when they are righteous (1 Nephi 13:34–35). Thus, the emphasis of Church prophets to Church members is to spread the Book of Mormon and its message to the citizens of this land. That was the vision of President Ezra Taft Benson ("Flooding the Earth with the Book of Mormon," 4–6).

It is true that the Gentiles knew about Christ before the Restoration commenced. The Bible, especially the New Testament, contains the requirements necessary to be a follower of Jesus Christ and outlines the responsibilities that come with discipleship. Recall that the covenant on the land has to do with obeying the "God of the land, who is Jesus Christ" (Ether 2:12). Most of the early settlers were God-fearing people who brought with them the biblical text. The early Reformers, who broke from the Catholic tradition, succeeded in getting the Bible into the hands of the common people. The invention of the printing press allowed the sacred text to be printed and placed in the hands of individuals other than clergy. Nephi makes a point of the biblical record being carried to this land by the Gentiles (1 Nephi 13:20–29; 32). Thus, as a people the settlers were free to practice Christian principles as they are found in the Bible. Latter-day Saints are to share with the Gentiles and all others the message of the Book of Mormon along with the doctrines of the Restoration. One of the three-fold missions of the Church is to take the gospel to all the world. The Book of Mormon restores the simple doctrines and principles of the gospel along with the covenants that God establishes with His children

An angel outlined to Nephi the promises and consequences that the Gentiles faced as they settled the very land where the gospel was to be restored. Those promises and consequences were based on their being aware of the Book of Mormon record:

> And it shall come to pass, that if the Gentiles shall hearken unto the Lamb of God in that day that he shall manifest himself unto them in word and also in power, in very deed, unto the taking away of their stumbling blocks—
>
> And harden not their hearts against the Lamb of God, they shall be numbered among the seed of thy father; yea, they shall be numbered among the house of Israel; and they shall be a blessed people upon the promised land *forever;* they shall be no

more brought down into captivity; and the house of Israel shall no more be confounded. . . .

Therefore, wo be unto the Gentiles if is so be that they harden their hearts against the Lamb of God.

For the time cometh, saith the Lamb of God, that I will work a great and a marvelous work among the children of men; a work which shall be everlasting, either on the one hand or on the other—either to the convincing of them unto peace and life eternal, or unto the deliverance of them to the hardness of their hearts and the blindness of their minds unto their being brought down into captivity, and also into destruction, both temporally and spiritually. (1 Nephi 14:1–7; italics added)

The Gentiles are accountable to God for their behavior to the extent that they have the Old and New Testaments. They have done a great work in getting this nation underway. This is their day, the day of the Gentile, the dispensation of the fulness of times (D&C 45:28–30; 112:30; 128:20).

Although the Gentiles have great promises extended to them if they will accept the gospel, Nephi saw that one major problem the Church would face in the last days was "priestcraft," wherein clergy "preach and set themselves up for a light unto the world, that they may get gain and praise of the world; but they seek not the welfare of Zion" (2 Nephi 26:29). Priestcraft has prevented many from coming into the true fold of God as their minds have been poisoned concerning Joseph Smith and the Restoration. As the Church moves forward "out of obscurity and out of darkness" (D&C 1:30), however, and as our missionary force increases, as our people become leaders in government and business, and as the Saints live the gospel, honest truth seekers among the Gentiles will be attracted to the restored gospel. We are reminded once again of the words of President Boyd K. Packer:

Across the world, those who now come by the tens of thousands will inevitably come as a flood to where the family is safe. Here they will worship the Father in the name of Christ, by the gift of the Holy Ghost, and know that the gospel is the great plan of happiness, of redemption, of which I bear witness. ("Father and the Family," 21)

Jacob explained that "the Gentiles shall be blessed upon the land. And this land shall be a land of liberty unto the Gentiles, and there shall be no kings upon the land, who shall raise up unto the Gentiles. And I will fortify this land against all other nations" (2 Nephi 10:10–12).

Jesus, in his visit to the Nephites, talked about the latter-day inhabitants of this land and of the Book of Mormon record that would come forth among them and be taken to the seed of Lehi:

> For it is wisdom in the Father that they should be established in this land, and be set up as a free people by the power of the Father, that these things might come forth from them unto a remnant of your seed, that the covenant of the Father may be fulfilled which he hath covenanted with his people, O house of Israel. (3 Nephi 21:4)

The Savior then explained how the gospel would go forth from the Gentiles to the latter-day remnant of the people to whom He was speaking:

> Therefore, when these works and the works which shall be wrought among you hereafter shall come forth from the Gentiles unto your seed which shall dwindle in unbelief because of iniquity;
>
> For thus it behooveth the Father that it should come forth from the Gentiles, that he may show forth his power unto the Gentiles, for this cause that the Gentiles, if they will not harden

their hearts, that they may repent and come unto me and be baptized in my name and know of the true points of my doctrine, that they may be numbered among my people, O house of Israel. (3 Nephi 21:5–6)

That remnant, as we have seen, is the Lamanite. As Latter-day Saints, we know of the promises made to the Gentiles. Mormon refers to Church members among the Gentiles as those who "have care for the house of Israel, that realize and know from whence their blessings come. For I know that such will sorrow for the calamity of the house of Israel" (Mormon 5:10–11). Although wonderful promises are extended to the Gentiles, the problem of pride, that old Nephite disease, would cause major problems with their spirituality. It seems that whenever people gain political freedom, find that labor-saving devices leave them with an abundance of leisure time, when thy enjoy economic prosperity, and a plethora of goods and services are readily available, the dangers of spiritual apathy and pride seem to crowd out humility and meekness. For this reason, Mormon called the Gentiles to repentance (3 Nephi 30).

The Gentiles, because of their belief in Christ, are under a covenant similar to that of the earlier inhabitants of the land. Joseph Smith's first vision, wherein both God the Father and His Son Jesus Christ visited the young Prophet as a prelude to the Restoration, came forth in this land of promise and invites their investigation. The Book of Mormon, a book written for them, is now available to them in many languages (Book of Mormon Title Page).[1]

Historically, the Lord blessed and protected this nation from the ravages of war and economic disaster that might otherwise have led to the destruction of the nation. The Civil War came close to destroying the nation, but with a humble president who sought inspiration and wisdom from God, the nation survived the most serious challenge to its continuity. God has had a hand in the affairs of this land. President Ezra Taft Benson taught:

> When this nation was established, the Church was restored and from here the message of the restored gospel has gone forth—all according to divine plan. This then becomes the Lord's base of operations in these latter days. . . .
>
> It was His latter-day purpose to bring forth His gospel in America, not in any other place. It was in America where the Book of Mormon plates were deposited. That was no accident. It was His design. (*Teachings of Ezra Taft Benson,* 571)

Stage 3: God Establishes Laws for the Goverance of the People

The legal system of the United States has been the envy of other nations, and a number of countries have modeled their own constitution after ours. The Lord revealed to Joseph Smith, during a particularly intense period of persecution, that the Saints were to

> importune for redress, and redemption, by the hands of those who are placed as rulers and are in authority over you—
>
> According to the laws and constitution of the people, which I have suffered to be established, and should be maintained for the rights and protection of all flesh, according to just and holy principles. . . .
>
> And for this purpose have I established the Constitution of this land, by the hands of wise men whom I raised up unto this very purpose. (D&C 101:76–80)

Joseph Smith observed, "The Constitution is not a law, but it empowers the people to make laws" (*Teachings of the Prophet Joseph Smith,* 278). Thus the Constitution became a guide for fair and equitable lawmaking by the Congress. This inspired document has stood the test of time. When matters of law are appealed to the highest court in the land, the Supreme Court, nine judges in the court of last resort, are to make decisions on the cases that come before them based on the merits of a law as it can or cannot be supported by principles found in the Constitution. Of course, the judges themselves can be tainted by the philosophies of men and by their own moral compass which they acquired growing up in the very civilization where they are to make judgments. Thus, we are now hearing decisions from that court which go contrary to what "the God of the land, who is Jesus Christ," would desire (Ether 2:12). For example, to interpret the Constitution as supporting the killing of the unborn through abortion on demand is a decision that could only come in a society that has lost its spiritual moorings. Immoral behavior sustained by legal fiat is contrary to the will of God as revealed to his prophets and as found in the scriptures. To interpret the Constitution of the United States as supporting abortion is contrary to the Christian principles upon which this nation was founded. To interpret the Constitution as being against religious observances and practices of all kinds, even in public settings, as it has been of late, is an indication of faulty logic and misinterpretation of what the Founding Fathers had in mind. We live in an age of activist judges who, rather than simply interpreting law so that the people can decide if more or less legislation is needed, have turned to *making* laws themselves by mandating enforcement of their own interpretations.[2]

Given our early history of persecution as a Church, of members being driven from their homes, cities, and states, Joseph Smith observed that the Constitution was not always used properly to protect minorities:

The only fault I find with the Constitution is, it is not broad enough to cover the whole ground.

Although it provides that all men shall enjoy religious freedom, yet it does not provide the manner by which that freedom can be preserved, nor for the punishment of Government officers who refuse to protect the people in their religious rights, or punish those mobs, states, or communities who interfere with the rights of the people on account of their religion. Its sentiments are good, but it provides no means of enforcing them. It has but this one fault." (*Teachings of the Prophet Joseph Smith*, 326–27)

Ironically, the very Prophet of the Restoration was killed in a society in which his life should have been preserved by the Constitution.

Stage 4: When Most of the People Choose Evil over Good, the Covenant Is Breached

Are the majority of the inhabitants of this land presently choosing evil over good? Do they prefer wickedness to righteousness? Recall King Mosiah's declaration: "And if the time comes that the *voice of the people doth choose iniquity, then is the time that the judgments of God will come upon you; yea, then is the time he will visit you with great destruction* even as he has hitherto visited this land" (Mosiah 29:27; italics added). As long as most of the people sustain the laws of the land and live in harmony with the principles of acceptable Judeo-Christian conduct, the nation will prosper. This righteous king also taught that "it is not common that the voice of the people desireth anything contrary to that which is right; but it is common for the lesser part of the people to desire that which is not right; therefore this shall ye observe and make it your law—to do your business by the voice of the people" (Mosiah 29:26).

Our nation is composed of people from different philosophical and political camps. There are those who feel the country has never been in better shape. There are those, as measured by the nightly news and talk shows, who think the nation is on the verge of collapse. But the Lord, the supreme Judge and Evaluator, outlined in principle that the majority of people who live upon this land cannot become an evil, wicked population and retain their right to live here. The inhabitants are to support the principles espoused in the gospel of Jesus Christ. There is no room for immorality, for dishonesty, for graft of corruption, for abuse, or for any other practice that runs counter to the principles of Christian living.

As an exercise in evaluating the spirituality of the nation's citizens as a whole, let us consider several important issues. How does the majority of people in this land feel about these issues? How does the God of the land, Jesus Christ, view them?

1. Abortion on demand
2. The Sabbath day as a day of worship
3. Consenting adults being sexually involved (adultery, fornication, homosexual liaisons)
4. Living together without a legal marriage
5. Acknowledging God in public—prayer, the Ten Commandments
6. Same-gender marriage or civil union
7. Abuse of children, spouse, elderly
8. Dishonest business practices
9. Honesty in paying tithing, taxes
10. Alcohol, drug use
11. Cursing, swearing, taking the Lord's name in vain
12. Divorce, broken homes
13. Pornography, R-rated movies
14. Violence in the media, gangs, rape
15. Rudeness, manners, road rage, criticism, complaining

16. Failure to vote, to serve on juries, or to carry out other responsibilities of citizenship in the land of promise

17. The need for the Ten Commandments

18. Sportsmanship

19. Euthanasia

20. Personal anger, temper

21. Morality of public servants

As we think about matters of this kind, we begin to see that there has been some major spiritual slippage under Gentile leadership. Certainly the foregoing are not of equal value, but they indicate some of the issues that are weakening the spiritual foundations of this land. We must ask ourselves: Have we passed the point beyond which the majority of Americans are on the side of evil? Does the majority support views that are contrary to what God requires of the inhabitants of this land? It could be argued that these issues, taken together, reflect a measure of the spirituality of our nation. The Lord, of course, assesses when the majority of people choose evil over good. He knows when people need a reminder of the responsibilities that accompany the blessings of freedom.

The future of America does not depend on what political party is in control of the White House or the Congress; rather, *the righteousness of the people themselves* determines whether we have the blessings of heaven as a nation. We cannot be blessed if we are living contrary to the principles of the gospel of Jesus Christ.

Stage 5: The Lord Warns the Inhabitants When They Are in Danger of Being Swept Off

In 1974, President Spencer W. Kimball, for the first time in this final dispensation, called every worthy young man into missionary service.[3] What does such a call from the Lord's prophet mean? Let's put it in perspective. If the nation's president were to call all able-bodied men into the military (as was done in World War II), it would be assumed that a serious threat to the peace and stability of the nation existed. So, likewise, when a prophet of God calls every worthy and prepared young man into the mission field, that is an indication that the spiritual welfare of the country (and the world) is in a serious decline. The ripening process is well underway. As a missionary church, we have two important responsibilities:

1. We must share the message that the gospel of Jesus Christ and His priesthood have been restored to the earth. New scriptures have come forth that are written to the inhabitants of the earth, especially to those who live on this land. These scriptures warn of the consequences of disobedience to the fundamental laws of God.

2. We must be a warning voice to the people of this land as well as of the world that the judgments of God are looming if His laws are continually broken. The ripening process is moving this nation toward the edge of the precipice. Similarly, other nations will be accountable for their level of understanding of the laws of God (Alma 20:8). The call to repentance has gone forth to all nations. As president of the Quorum of the Twelve Apostles, in 1975 President Ezra Taft Benson warned:

> As humble servants of the Lord, we call upon the leaders of nations to humble themselves before God, to seek his inspiration and guidance. We call upon rulers and people alike to repent of their evil ways. Turn unto the Lord, seek his forgiveness, and unite yourselves in humility with his kingdom. There is no other way. If you will do this, your sins will be blotted out, peace will come and remain, and you will become a part of the kingdom of God in preparation for Christ's second coming. But if you refuse to repent or to accept the testimony of his inspired messengers and unite yourselves with God's kingdom,

then the terrible judgments and calamities promised the wicked will be yours.

The Lord in his mercy has provided a way of escape. The voice of warning is to all people by the mouths of his servants. If this voice is not heeded, the angels of destruction will increasingly go forth, and the chastening hand of Almighty God will be felt upon the nations, as decreed, until a full end thereof will be the result. Wars, devastation, and untold suffering will be your lot except you turn unto the Lord in humble repentance. Destruction, even more terrible and far-reaching than attended the last great war, will come with certainty unless rulers and people alike repent and cease their evil and godless ways. God will not be mocked. He will not permit the sins of sexual immorality, secret murderous combinations, the killing of the unborn, and disregard for all his holy commandments and the messages of his servants to go unheeded without grievous punishments for such wickedness. The nations of the world cannot endure in sin. The way of escape is clear. The immutable laws of God remain steadfastly in the heavens above. When men and nations refuse to abide by them, the penalty must follow. They will be wasted away. Sin demands punishment. ("Message to the World," 32)

The call to every young man to enter the missionary force has been possible only in the past quarter-century when there has been no mandatory military service, or draft. When wartime conditions require the nation's youth to bear arms, it is impossible for every young man to serve a mission because the draft usually begins at age eighteen. During the Korean and Vietnam wars, for example, the number of missionaries from each ward was curtailed. Now, however, every worthy young man can carry out the divine mandate to take the gospel to the entire world. We have been truly blessed as a people economically and politically. We have the ability at the present time to generate sufficient resources to send every worthy young man who will go. We are, from a historical perspective, living in a time when, without a military draft, the window of opportunity allows our worthy and spiritually, physically, and emotionally healthy young men to take the gospel to the world.

The extent of the warning message of the Lord's servants depends on the spiritual level of people. If people are wicked, if they are ripe in iniquity, if the judgments of God are nearing, then the message will be stern and threatening, as it was in Enoch's day (Moses 7:10).

Noah likewise warned the people of his generation: "Believe and repent of your sins and be baptized in the name of Jesus Christ, the Son of God, even as our fathers, and ye shall receive the Holy Ghost; . . . and if ye do not this, the floods will come in upon you" (Moses 8:24).

The prophet Samuel declared to the Nephites:

> Ye do not remember the Lord your God in the things with which he hath blessed you, but ye do always remember your riches, not to thank the Lord your God for them; yea, your hearts are not drawn out unto the Lord, but they do swell with great pride, unto boasting, and unto great swelling, envyings, strifes, malice, persecutions, and murders, and all manner of iniquities.
>
> For this cause hath the Lord God caused that a curse should come upon the land, and also upon your riches, and this because of your iniquities. (Helaman 13:22–23)

We are now moving forward in a new millennium, but our message to the world is not yet one of hellfire and destruction. Rather, our missionaries call on people in their homes and in the streets to invite them to listen to a message about the Savior. Yet relatively few people care enough to really want to know more about the gospel. If they do not want to hear our message, we quietly and respectfully leave without dusting off our feet. Many good people still abide in the land, and there are people who will listen to our message of hope. Decent and wholesome people outside the Church contribute a positive effect to the social order. The ripening process has not reached the point of threatening judgments of death and destruction to anyone—yet. Many Christians, Jews, Lamanites, and Muslims still believe in the dignity of mankind. They sustain order and participate in the political process, believe in a Supreme Being, and oppose efforts to take God out of the pledge of allegiance and His name from our coins and paper money. They insist that the Constitution be upheld. Many people love their spouses and their children. So we are not to the point—yet—where the prophets are threatening imminent destruction. Specific calamities are not being pronounced by the servants of God at the moment. The Lord's prophets still are able to travel the country and the world teaching, building, and lifting others with inspiring messages of encouragement. The Saints are prospering, and so are the Gentiles. We are in a period of tolerance and acceptance that allows Latter-day Saints to practice their religion without threat of incarceration, death, or serious persecution by those whom we seek to enlighten.

But who cannot see the ripening process among the Gentiles? We are not blind to the immoral behavior and the political and corporate corruption taking place. Shockingly, more people now live together without being married than we have members of the Church worldwide! Immoral lyrics and media messages abound. Lifestyles offensive to God proliferate. President Gordon B. Hinckley spoke of the ripening processes going on in our land:

> Never before, at least not in our generation, have the forces of evil been so blatant, so brazen, so aggressive as they are today. Things we dared not speak about in earlier times are now constantly projected into our living rooms. All sensitivity is cast

aside as reporters and pundits speak with a disgusting plainness of things that can only stir curiosity and lead to evil.

Some to whom we have looked as leaders have betrayed us. We are disappointed and disillusioned. And their activity is only the tip of the iceberg. In successive layers beneath that tip is a great mass of sleaze and filth, of dissolute and dishonest behavior." ("Walking in the Light of the Lord," 98–99)

Prophets define where we are in the ripening process. It is to them that we look to find out how we are doing as a Church, as a nation, and as a world community. The growth of the Church in recent times has been spectacular, and general conference messages in past decades have been, for the most part, upbeat and positive. They have spoken with appreciation for the faithfulness of the Saints and their generosity and faithfulness in paying tithing, building temples, serving missions, researching family history, giving humanitarian aid, contributing to educational programs, and donating means and time to serve in a lay church. But interlaced with those comments are concerns about our commitment to share the gospel, about the need for more older couples to serve missions, and about the necessity for all to avoid offensive media presentations and to flee from pornography and other evils that are a large part of the Gentile culture and against which we are not immune.

Stage 6: The Inhabitants Respond to the Warnings from God's Servants

The inhabitants of the land who are warned must choose their response: Will they accept the warning? Reject it? Tolerate it? We might ask, How well is our message being received? As, hopefully, the number of missionaries serving in the field increases, does the number of converts increase? Are more people accepting the message of the gospel? The accompanying chart indicates the number of full-time missionaries and converts to the Church in recent years (statistics from Conference Report for the April following each designated year).

Year	Missionaries	Converts
1990	43,651	330,877
1991	43,395	297,770
1992	46,025	274,477
1993	48,708	304,808
1994	47,311	300,730
1995	48,631	304,330
1996	52,938	321,385
1997	56,531	317,398
1998	57,853	299,134
1999	58,593	306,171
2000	60,784	273,973
2001	61,638	283,138
2002	60,850	292,612
2003	56,237	242,923
2004	51,067	241,239

In the last decade or so, Latter-day Saints have consistently averaged one-fourth to one-third of a million converts worldwide each year. Our missionary force is becoming more effective in teaching the gospel, and we are concerned about retaining those who join the Church. Temples are springing up worldwide. The Saints, in general, have been blessed financially by a combination of economic stability and relatively low unemployment. But underneath the recent eras of prosperity (there will always be recessions and those who suffer financially even in good times) and increased productivity, the popularity of obscene movies, raucous music, and vulgar lyrics, use of the

Internet to view pornography, immoral presentations on television, blatant messages about same-gender sex, and heterosexuals living together without marriage offend the ears and hearts of those who know and love the gospel of Jesus Christ.

When people reject the gospel, they live without the added light of revelation. If individuals are not interested in seeking truth about Heavenly Father and His plan of salvation, apathy and pride bring about selfishness, greed, and hopelessness. As morale declines, it becomes more difficult to share the message of the restoration because of the wickedness and evil that exists among the people. "The love of men shall wax cold, and iniquity shall abound," said the Lord to His latter-day prophet (D&C 45:27). Moroni spoke to those who were apathetic, who care not for truth, and who, when they are taught the gospel, lack the courage to accept it and implement it: "For the time speedily cometh that ye shall know that I lie not, for ye shall see me at the bar of God; and the Lord God will say unto you: Did I not declare my words unto you, which were written by this man, like as one crying from the dead, yea, even as one speaking out of the dust?" (Moroni 10:27). The day will come when those who are not willing to listen, who are not willing to seek truth, will be held accountable for their decisions. To the terrestrial kingdom go those "who received not the testimony of Jesus in the flesh, but afterwards received it" (D&C 76:74).

As committed Latter-day Saints, on the other hand, we must exercise a spirit of charity in dealing with those not of our faith. In today's world, people are mobile and preoccupied. Two missionaries who knock at the door during dinner or when a baby is crying may not find that moment the most propitious time for the residents to stop what they are doing and listen to two strangers. Most people are apathetic about religion, and in a day of burglaries, questionable salespersons appearing at one's door, busy schedules, some antipathy or disillusionment toward religion (televangelists clamoring for dollars), the false assumption that it doesn't matter which church you belong to as long as you have "orthodox" Christian beliefs, gives little incentive to people to listen to the missionaries. The attitude of "My grandfather was a _____, my parents were _____, and I am not going to change" contributes to a lack of interest in searching for spiritual truth.

But people cannot be condemned if a knock at the door is their only means of learning about the Church. Hopefully, as world events change, as economic realities change, as wickedness in the world obviously ripens before their eyes, as more and more judgments command the attention of people, and as people are forced to reexamine their lives, they will seek spiritual meaning, seek answers to questions concerning Deity and the purposes of life. We hope that as Latter-day Saints, we will play a role in causing people to examine their lives and belief in God and desire to know the truth about religious thought and practices. The Church, through radio and television advertisements, sends messages into Gentile homes because guarded gates often prevent missionaries from reaching doors.

> And ye are called to bring to pass the gathering of mine elect; for mine elect hear my voice and harden not their hearts;
> Wherefore the decree hath gone forth from the Father that they shall be gathered in unto one place upon the face of this land, to prepare their hearts and be prepared in all things against the day when tribulation and desolation are sent forth upon the wicked. (D&C 29:7–8)

As Latter-day Saints, we have a duty to live by example and by word to attract people to the gospel. Most people show an interest in the Church when they have met members of the Church whom they respect. When the majority of a people rejects the message and the messengers, the society moves to Stage 7.

Stage 7: When the People Reject Prophetic Warnings, the Judgments of God Begin

The Gentiles have two options: accept the gospel and participate in the building of the Lord's kingdom in the latter-days or continue in wickedness to such an extent that the judgments of God will destroy them. The Lord discussed this issue during his visit to the Nephites:

> *And blessed are the Gentiles, because of their belief in me,* in and of the Holy Ghost, which witnesses unto them of me and of the Father.
>
> Behold, because of their belief in me, saith the Father, and because of the unbelief of you, O house of Israel, in the latter day shall the truth come unto the Gentiles, *that the fulness of these things shall be made known unto them.*
>
> But wo, saith the Father, unto the unbelieving of the Gentiles—for notwithstanding they have come forth upon the face of this land, and have scattered my people who are of the house of Israel; . . .
>
> And because of the mercies of the Father unto the Gentiles, and also the judgments of the Father upon my people who are of the house of Israel, verily, verily, I say unto you, that after all this, and I have caused my people who are of the house of Israel to be smitten, and to be afflicted, and to be slain, and to be cast out from among them, and to become hated by them, and to become a hiss and a byword among them—
>
> And thus commandeth the Father that I should say unto you: At that day when the Gentiles shall sin against my gospel, and shall reject the fulness of my gospel, and shall be lifted up in the pride of their hearts above all nations, and above all the people of the whole earth, and shall be filled with all manner of lyings, and of deceits, and of mischiefs, and all manner of hypocrisy, and murders, and priestcrafts, and whoredoms, and

of secret abominations; and if they shall do all those things, and shall reject the fulness of my gospel, behold, saith the Father, I will bring the fulness of my gospel from among them. . . .

But if the Gentiles will repent and return unto me, saith the Father, behold they shall be numbered among my people, O house of Israel. (3 Nephi 16:6–13; italics added)

To reject the message of the prophets and missionaries is to bring the judgments of God upon the land. Such judgments have historically come as natural disasters—famine, earthquake, pestilence—as well as war and economic downturns. Numerous prophecies concerning the future of this land exist. The Lord told the Prophet Joseph Smith:

For not many days hence and the earth shall tremble and reel to and fro as a drunken man; and the sun shall hide his face, and shall refuse to give light; and the moon shall be bathed in blood; and the stars shall become exceedingly angry, and shall cast themselves down as a fig that falleth from off a fig-tree.

And after your testimony cometh wrath and indignation upon the people. (D&C 88:87–88)

The Lord indicated that the day would come when

there shall be weeping and wailing among the hosts of men;

And there shall be a great hailstorm sent forth to destroy the crops of the earth.

And it shall come to pass, because of the wickedness of the world, that I will take vengeance upon the wicked, for they will not repent; for the cup of mine indignation is full; for behold, my blood shall not cleanse them if they hear me not. (D&C 29:15–17)

In a general conference address years ago, before the "ripening process" was as far along as it is now, Elder Spencer W. Kimball assessed the attitude of people in this modern age:

Jesus Christ our Lord is under no obligation to save this world. The people have ignored him, disbelieved him, failed to follow him. They stand at his mercy which will be extended only if they repent. But to what extent have we repented? Another prophet said, "We call evil good, and good evil." Men have rationalized themselves into thinking that they are "not so bad." Are they fully ripe? Has the rot of age and flabbiness set in? Can they change? They see evil in their enemies, but none in themselves. Even in the true Church numerous of its people fail to attend their meetings, to tithe their incomes, to have their regular prayers, to keep all the commandments. We can transform, but will we? It seems that we would rather tax ourselves into slavery than to pay our tithes; rather build protections and walls than drop to our knees with our families in solemn prayers night and morning.

It seems that rather than fast and pray, we prefer to gorge ourselves at the banquet tables and drink cocktails. Instead of disciplining ourselves, we yield to urges and carnal desires. Numerous billions we spend on liquor and tobacco. A Sabbath show or a game or a race replaces solemn worship. Numerous mothers prefer the added luxuries of two incomes to the satisfactions of seeing children grow up in the fear of God. Men golf and boat and hunt and fish rather than to solemnize the Sabbath. Old man rationalization is with us. Because we are not vicious enough to be confined in penitentiaries, we rationalize that we are pretty good people; that we are not doing so badly. ("Listen to the Prophet's Voice," 938)

Stage 8: The Spirit of the Lord Withdraws from the People

Of course, wickedness of individuals or nations causes a withdrawal of the Lord's Spirit. When a nation ripens in iniquity, as we have seen with the Jaredites and Nephites, the influence of the Spirit of the Lord is diminished. Our making a judgment about divine judgments at this point is difficult because our society has a great many people who champion and promote Christian ideals. The fruit is not yet ready to be cast out. Joseph Smith wrote to the editor of a newspaper:

> For some length of time I have been carefully viewing the state of things, as it now appears, throughout our Christian land; and have looked at it with feelings of the most painful anxiety. While upon one hand I behold the manifest withdrawal of God's Holy Spirit; upon the other hand, I behold the judgments of God that have swept, and are still sweeping hundreds and thousands of our race, and I fear unprepared, down to the shades of death. . . .
>
> . . . the Gentiles have not continued in the goodness of God, but have departed from the faith that was once delivered to the Saints, and have broken the covenant in which their fathers were established (see Isaiah xxiv:5); and have become high-minded, and have not feared; therefore, but few of them will be gathered with the chosen family. Have not the pride, high-mindedness, and unbelief of the Gentiles, provoked the Holy One of Israel to withdraw His Holy Spirit from them, and send forth His judgments to scourge them for their wickedness? This is certainly the case. (*Teachings of the Prophet Joseph Smith,* 13–15)

Individually, people live their lives along a continuum from righteousness to extreme wickedness. Many individuals and organizations understand the significance of the decline of morality in this land. Wonderful people in our nation have a sense of decency and desire wholesome influences in their lives. On the other hand, we also live in an age of easy access to pornography and visual media repugnant to the Spirit of the Lord and offensive to Christlike people. When efforts have been made to curb the gross filth and wicked behaviors portrayed in movies, the cry of "censorship" goes up. And with the courts ruling in favor of freedom of speech and the right to publish indecent material, the moral backbone of this nation has slipped dramatically. Elder Boyd K. Packer has said:

> Today I speak to members of the Church as an environmentalist. My message is not on the *physical* but on the *moral and spiritual environment* in which we must raise our families. As we test the *moral* environment, we find the *pollution* index is spiraling upward. . . .
>
> The rapid, sweeping deterioration of values is characterized by a preoccupation—even an obsession—with the procreative act. Abstinence before marriage and fidelity within it are openly scoffed at—marriage and parenthood ridiculed as burdensome, unnecessary. Modesty, a virtue of a refined individual or society, is all but gone.
>
> The adversary is jealous toward all who have the power to beget life. He cannot beget life; he is impotent. . . .
>
> With ever fewer exceptions, what we see and read and hear have the mating act as a central theme. Censorship is forced offstage as a violation of individual freedom.
>
> That which should be absolutely private is disrobed and acted out center stage. In the shadows backstage are addiction, pornography, perversion, infidelity, abortion, and—the saddest of them all—incest and molestation. In company with them now is a plague of biblical proportion. And all of them are on the increase.
>
> Society excuses itself from responsibility except for teaching the physical process of reproduction to children in school to prevent pregnancy and disease, and providing teenagers with devices which are supposed to protect them from both.
>
> When any effort is made to include values in these courses, basic universal values, not just values of the Church, but of

civilization, of society itself, the protest arises, "You are impos-
ing religion upon us, infringing upon our freedom."

While we pass laws to reduce pollution of the earth, any pro-
posal to protect the moral and spiritual environment is shouted
down and marched against as infringing upon liberty, agency,
freedom, the right to choose.

Interesting how one virtue, when given exaggerated or fanat-
ical emphasis, can be used to batter down another, with freedom, a virtue, invoked to protect *vice*. Those determined to
transgress see any regulation of their life-style as interfering with
their agency and seek to have their actions condoned by making them legal. ("Our Moral Environment," 66)

The Savior told Joseph Smith that "as it was in the days of Noah,
so it shall be also at the coming of the Son of Man" (Joseph
Smith–Matthew 1:41). In Noah's day, "the wickedness of men had
become great in the earth; and *every man* was lifted up in the imagination of the thoughts of his heart, being only evil continually"
(Moses 8:22; italics added). If that extreme condition comes again in
our day, it will be sad for us, for when men and women reach a certain level of thinking and behavior that has little room for goodness
and decency, society cannot survive long on this land.

Stage 9: The Inhabitants Become Fully Ripened in Iniquity and Cast Out the Righteous

The ripening of fruit proceeds in only one direction. The Lord
told Joseph Smith in modern times, "Behold, the world is ripening in
iniquity; and it must needs be that the children of men are stirred up
unto repentance, both the Gentiles and also the house of Israel"
(D&C 18:6). Again, He said, "For the hour is nigh and the day soon
at hand when the earth is ripe; and all the proud and they that do

wickedly shall be as stubble; and I will burn them up, saith the Lord of Hosts, that wickedness shall not be upon the earth" (D&C 29:9). In the Doctrine and Covenants, the Lord states that "in that place they shall lift up their voices unto God against that people, yea, unto him whose anger is kindled against their wickedness, a people who are well-nigh ripened for destruction" (D&C 61:31). In the coming days, the ripening process will be hastened.

The wicked seek legal means to shut the mouths of the righteous. Once again, we see lies and distortions about those with religious motives. Using the label "religious right," many attempt to make religious people appear as fanatics or radicals. When such attacks fail, the wicked move to forcibly cast the righteous out of their presence, as they did with the Nephites before the coming of the Lord to them. But the Lord will not tolerate His people being cast aside by the wicked as long as they are doing their best to obey His will. He will fight their battles when there are sufficient numbers of righteous saints. This time He will not need to lead away a righteous colony as he did with the Jaredites, Mulekites, and Lehites because the Saints will be of sufficient number and righteousness for the Lord to intervene in their behalf.

After seeing in vision events of the last days and commenting on Isaiah's prophecies, Nephi said of the latter days:

> For the time soon cometh that the fulness of the wrath of God shall be poured out upon all the children of men; for he will not suffer that the wicked shall destroy the righteous.
>
> Wherefore, he will preserve the righteous by his power, even if it so be that the fulness of his wrath must come, and the righteous be preserved, even unto the destruction of their enemies by fire. Wherefore, the righteous need not fear; for thus saith the prophet, they shall be saved, even if it so be as by fire.
>
> . . . I say unto you, that these things must shortly come; yea, even blood, and fire, and vapor of smoke must come; and it

must needs be upon the face of this earth; and it cometh unto men according to the flesh if it so be that they will harden their hearts against the Holy One of Israel.

For behold, the righteous shall not perish; for the time surely must come that all they who fight against Zion shall be cut off. . . .

And the righteous need not fear, for they are those who shall not be confounded. But it is the kingdom of the devil, which shall be built up among the children of men . . .

. . . ; yea, in fine, all those who belong to the kingdom of the devil are they who need fear, and tremble, and quake; they are those who must be brought low in the dust; they are those who must be consumed as stubble . . .

And the time cometh speedily that the righteous must be led up as calves of the stall, and the Holy One of Israel must reign in dominion, and might, and power, and great glory. (1 Nephi 22:16–24)

Then Nephi spoke of millennial conditions:

And because of the righteousness of his people, Satan has no power; wherefore, he cannot be loosed for the space of many years; for he hath no power over the hearts of the people, for they dwell in righteousness, and the Holy One of Israel reigneth. . . .

But, behold, all nations, kindreds, tongues, and people shall dwell safely in the Holy One of Israel if it so be that they will repent. (1 Nephi 22:26–28)

Nephi outlined the choices available to the Gentiles: "Wo be unto the Gentiles, saith the Lord God of Hosts! For notwithstanding I shall lengthen out mine arm unto them from day to day, they will deny me; nevertheless, I will be merciful unto them, saith the Lord God, if they will repent and come unto me; for mine arm is lengthened out all the day long, saith the Lord God of Hosts" (2 Nephi 28:32). And again, "as many of the Gentiles as will repent are the covenant people of the Lord" (2 Nephi 30:2). As Latter-day Saints, we can perhaps delay the onset of this stage or even prevent it. Elder Bruce R. McConkie taught:

> If we, as a people, keep the commandments of God; if we take the side of the Church on all issues, both religious and political; if we take the Holy Spirit for our guide; if we give heed to the words of the apostles and prophets who minister among us—then, from an eternal standpoint, all things will work together for our good.
>
> Our view of the future shall be undimmed, and, whether in life or in death, we shall see our blessed Lord return to reign on earth. We shall see the New Jerusalem coming down from God in heaven to join with the Holy City we have built. We shall mingle with those of Enoch's city while together we worship and serve the Lord forever.[4]

Stage 10: The Wicked Are Destroyed

Perhaps the most tragic experience in the history of our own nation was the Civil War of the 1860s. More Americans were killed in that war than in any other we have fought. The number of war deaths in that tragedy were elevated because brother was fighting against brother—similar to the Jaredite and Nephite periods. The civil war that took place in this country did not result in a total annihilation of people as it did with the Jaredites and the Nephites, perhaps for three reasons:

1. Though the Saints were persecuted and driven beyond the boundaries of the United States, they found a new home in the West

and were able to increase their membership without the persecution they had previously experienced.

2. This nation was established by the Lord so that the gospel could go from its shores to the entire world. The Civil War humbled the people, and the nation recovered, just as the Nephites and the Jaredites had (3 Nephi 6:4–8; Ether 7:26; 9:34; 11:8). The Lord raised up an inspired, God-fearing president in Abraham Lincoln to hold this nation together during some very trying times. It was not meant that this land of America should be reduced to independent states as we find in Europe and in much of Africa.

3. The Saints, unfortunately, were not worthy to establish Zion at that time and deserved some rebuke. The Lord explained why the Saints were incapable of building Zion at that time (D&C 101:1–20; 103:1–14; 105:1–13). The righteousness and obedience of the Saints protected them from the ravages of the Civil War, but because they were not fully worthy to establish Zion, the Lord did not fight their battles. Thus, the Saints were humbled, but the Lord led them to a remote area of the promised land to build up the kingdom of God on the earth.

To issue an extermination order to drive the members of the Church out of Missouri, to commit atrocities against persons and possessions, were serious violations of the Constitution of the United States, which had been established by the Lord to protect this nation's citizens. The nation paid a severe penalty for driving the Saints out of the nation through ignorance, arrogance, and their own wickedness. The Lord told Brigham Young not many years before the American Civil War broke out:

> Thy brethren have rejected you and your testimony, even the nation that has driven you out;
> And now *cometh the day of their calamity,* even the days of sorrow, like a woman that is taken in travail; and their sorrow shall be great unless they speedily repent, yea, very speedily.

For they killed the prophets, and them that were sent unto them;
and they have shed innocent blood, which crieth from the ground
against them. (D&C 136:34–36; italics added)

The nation was punished for its belligerence and refusal to
address the calamities inflicted upon the Saints in Missouri and
Illinois. Elected officials sworn to uphold the principles of the
Constitution failed in their offices. In casting the Saints out of the
land, the Gentiles lost the Spirit of the Lord, and the Civil War came
close to destroying the Union.[5]

From the revelations of the Lord to Joseph Smith, it was made
known the Saints were not sufficiently righteous to establish Zion at
that time. The Lord was not pleased with the behavior of some members of the Church (D&C 105:3–5). Thus, while the Civil War took
a great toll on the inhabitants of the land, it was not a complete
destruction because the Saints were not fully worthy to establish
Zion.

Times have changed now, and the Saints are growing numeri-
cally in the land. If we are faithful to principle, we can provide a leav-
ening influence for good throughout the land. Many people will join
the Church because of our standards. We must have sufficient numbers and faithfulness among the Saints to carry out the work of the
last dispensation.

13

The Role of the
Latter-day Saints

What part do members of the Church play in the last days relative to the stages of decline that America faces and the threat of a divine broom? The ripening process is becoming more obvious in the larger culture. But what of the Saints who live among the Gentiles? What does the Lord expect of Church members now and in the days ahead? What have living prophets said about our influence, about our day, and about the impact we can have on the people and events of our time? Are Church members prepared to make a difference in the world in which we live, or have we become so enamored with the culture of the Gentiles that we have become like the Jews of Jesus' day? We think we are righteous because we carry our scriptures to church on the Sabbath, but perhaps we are not very knowledgeable about the doctrines of the Restoration. We have mental testimonies, but lack substance in our application of the gospel to everyday life.

Latter-day Saints have the important task, if they can, to convert the world to the message of the Restoration. That is the only way to preserve the Gentiles. Elder Joseph F. Smith warned the Saints:

I further testify, that unless the Latter-day Saints will live their religion, keep their covenants with God and their brethren, honor the priesthood which they bear, and try faithfully to bring themselves into subjection to the laws of God, they will be the first to fall beneath the judgments of the Almighty, *for his judgment will begin at his own house.* (Conference Report, April 1880, 96; italics added)

It appears that Latter-day Saints also face two options: We can be about our Father's business of sharing the gospel, preparing youth to serve missions, building strong marriages, constructing temples, and researching family histories (much more available to us now with the advent of computers). Or we can become intoxicated with the inventions, media, toys, and lifestyle of the Gentiles and sink ourselves into destruction.

The Lord explained to the Prophet Joseph Smith that the members of the Church must be faithful to their covenants and obligations or else they will be the *first to fall under His chastening hand:*

Vengeance cometh speedily upon the inhabitants of the earth, a day of wrath, a day of burning, a day of desolation, of weeping, of mourning, and of lamentation; and as a whirlwind it shall come upon all the face of the earth, saith the Lord.

And upon my house shall it begin, and from my house shall it go forth, saith the Lord;

First among those among you, saith the Lord, *who have professed to know my name and have not known me, and have blasphemed against me in the midst of my house,* saith the Lord. (D&C 112:24–26; italics added)

Simply being a member of the Church in these latter days will not be sufficient to survive the turbulent times ahead. The Lord will not bring judgments upon the wicked of the world if His own people have strayed; if they are not honoring their covenants. Having the fulness of the gospel, having been blessed with living prophets, apostles, latter-day scripture, and sermons available through television and radio transmission, the Internet, a variety of Church printed publications and other media offerings, and scriptural commentaries, leaves us little excuse to not be at our best in spreading the gospel worldwide.

Church History

The Church of Jesus Christ of Latter-day Saints began inauspiciously. On April 6, 1830, in Fayette, New York, six of the fifty-three individuals gathered in a small farmhouse officially incorporated the Church as a legal entity. The Book of Mormon had been published a week earlier. From such small and humble beginnings, the Church has grown rapidly. It now has members in practically every country of the free world. The future looks bright. In an address endorsed by President Spencer W. Kimball, Elder Bruce R. McConkie predicted that this work would roll forward to fulfill its worldwide destiny:

> We are living in a new day. The Church of Jesus Christ of Latter-day Saints is fast becoming a worldwide church. Congregations of Saints are now, or soon will be, strong enough to support and sustain their members no matter where they reside. Temples are being built wherever the need justifies. We can foresee many temples in South America in process of time.
>
> Stakes of Zion are also being organized at the ends of the earth." ("Come: Let Israel Build Zion," 117–18)

In its early days, the Church was driven from state to state and from pillar to post. It was forced to move from New York to Ohio, then to Missouri, and then to Illinois. The Saints were treated rudely by state officials and the local citizens until they were forced to move from Illinois to the Great Basin.[1] Establishing settlements in the Mountain West was a prodigious effort to form a bastion of safety and security far removed from the influence of those who would do the Church harm. The Saints settled in the tops of the mountains, as Isaiah foresaw (Isaiah 2:2–3). But even in this mountain retreat, they were threatened by the federal government's attempt to put down the "Utah rebellion," as it was called, when Johnston's army traveled west in 1857–58. From those dark and threatening days, however, we have grown to become an impressive people throughout the world. Our purpose in coming west was not to become hermits, for our mission extended to the world community. The mountains simply gave us space away from the Gentiles to become a people prepared to minister to the world. Our missionaries now have gone forth out of this sanctuary to every free nation of the world to carry the message of salvation to every soul who will listen

In the past hundred years or so, the Church has prospered in its journey "out of obscurity and out of darkness" (D&C 1:30). We now live in a day of respectability for the Church and its people generally. Our good works are beginning to catch the attention of the nations. Prophets travel the world to meet with governmental leaders and the Saints and encourage them to live the gospel and keep the Church membership in order. Temples have begun to dot the earth as we maintain some one hundred twenty such edifices worldwide, with more being planned. The national press gives the Church more positive coverage. Doors to more nations on every continent have been opened to us. Church leaders have built bridges of understanding with leaders and people of the free world. We now have a substantial number of Church members in the Congress. We have prominent men and women in positions of leadership in government, education, commerce, finance, banking, the judiciary, and medicine.

President Gordon B. Hinckley, reviewing the rise of the Church in these latter-days, concluded: "We stand on the summit of the ages, awed by a great and solemn sense of history. This is the last and final dispensation toward which all in the past has pointed." Then he predicted:

> And so we shall go forward on a continuing path of growth and progress and enlargement, touching for good the lives of people everywhere for as long as the earth shall last.
>
> At some stage in all of this onward rolling, Jesus Christ will appear to reign in splendor upon the earth. . . . It will be a welcome day. ("At the Summit of the Ages," 74)

We live in a remarkable age foreseen by prophets from the beginning of the world (D&C 121:26–28).

Modern Times

As the message of the Restoration spreads across the national and international landscape, our toughest confrontation is still with those whose religious thoughts are different from ours. We are not, in their minds, Christians. Joseph Smith's recital of his experience in the grove brought a rebuke from the clergy of his day who claimed that the heavens were closed and that divine manifestations were no longer possible. Our message as a Church has brought opposition in many quarters. The blame has not always been one-sided, however, as the Saints manifested their share of inadequacies.

The Lord explained to the Prophet Joseph Smith that He could not build Zion with the Saints of his day. For example, after the Saints' failure to build Zion in Missouri, the Lord responded when the Prophet made inquiry:

> I, the Lord, have suffered the affliction to come upon them, . . . in consequence of their transgressions. . . .
>
> Behold, I say unto you, there were jarrings, and contentions, and envyings, and strifes, and lustful and covetous desires

among them; therefore by these things they polluted their inheritances.

They were slow to hearken unto the voice of the Lord their God; therefore, the Lord their God is slow to hearken unto their prayers, to answer them in the day of their trouble.

In the day of their peace they esteemed lightly my counsel; but in the day of their trouble, of necessity they feel after me. (D&C 101:2–8)

In plain words, the Saints were not sufficiently united as a people to establish Zion. Later, as persecution mounted, the Prophet again petitioned the Lord for redress. The Lord answered:

I say unto you, were it not for the transgressions of my people, speaking concerning the church and not individuals they might have been redeemed even now.

But behold, they have not learned to be obedient to the things which I required at their hands, but are full of all manner of evil, and do not impart of their substance, as becometh saints, to the poor and afflicted among them. (D&C 105:2–3)

Then the Lord emphasized the overall problem, which was that His people

are not united according to the union required by the law of the celestial kingdom;

And Zion cannot be built up unless it is by the principles of the law of the celestial kingdom; otherwise I cannot receive her unto myself.

And my people must needs be chastened until they learn obedience, if it must needs be, by the things which they suffer. (D&C 105:4–6)

The early Saints were simply not prepared to accomplish the formidable task of building Zion, despite the desire of many of them to do so. The Lord explained that before they could succeed, before they could be spiritually and emotionally prepared, they would need to be endowed with power from on high, which could happen only after the temple in Kirtland was completed. With hindsight, we can see that early Church members had neither the experience, the maturity, nor the numbers to carry out this task.

The Church was forced to move again, this time to the banks of the Mississippi River in Illinois. There they drained the swampland and proceeded to build Nauvoo while seeking redress from the federal government and the state of Missouri for their recent losses. Their efforts were fruitless; both state and federal parties rejected the claims of the Saints and were unwilling to help—primarily because of political expedience. In Nauvoo the Saints built a temple that was the first sacred edifice to incorporate the ceremonies of the modern endowment, temple marriage, and sealing of families, the ordinances performed in present-day temples.

The redemption of Zion would have to wait until "my army become[s] very great, and let it be sanctified before me . . . ; that the kingdoms of this world may be constrained to acknowledge that the kingdom of Zion is in very deed the kingdom of our God and his Christ" (D&C 105:31–32).

We have come a long way since those early days of pioneering. The Church currently presents a robust picture of institutional health as the kingdom moves forward throughout the world under the direction of a Church organization poised to handle future growth. We are establishing congregations and houses of worship throughout the free world. Gone are the days, we hope, of being driven from homes and from the nation in which we live. We can now concentrate on spreading the gospel and its blessings to all of the Father's children. Apostles and prophets teach us of the Church's mission. We must do better this time than did the early Saints. Our coming to the West was done in order that the Saints "may be prepared, and that my people may be taught more perfectly, and have experience, and know more perfectly concerning their duty, and the things which I require at their hands" (D&C 105:10). We have learned much as a people since those early days.

Now we are taking advantage of the productivity and political safety of a great Gentile nation that once kicked us out of its borders. We are using technological developments and modern conveniences to take the gospel to the ends of the earth. The pioneers would have marveled at our present lifestyle. Prophets can now cross the country in less than a day, in contrast to months of plodding along in wagons or on horseback. Missionaries reach fields of labor in hours rather than days or weeks.

Prophets of old looked down the stream of time to our day. The Lord told Joseph Smith:

> God shall give unto you knowledge by his Holy Spirit, yea, by the unspeakable gift of the Holy Ghost, that has not been revealed since the world was until now;
>
> Which our forefathers have awaited with anxious expectation to be revealed in the last times, which their minds were pointed to by the angels as held in reserve for the fulness of their glory;
>
> A time to come in the which nothing shall be withheld, whether there be one God or many gods, they shall be manifest.
>
> All thrones and dominions, principalities and powers, shall be revealed and set forth upon all who have endured valiantly for the gospel of Jesus Christ. (D&C 121:26–29)

The Saints Are Accountable

As Church members preparing the earth for the Millennium requires spreading the gospel worldwide, establishing a righteous people, and redeeming the dead, we are making a solid effort to move the work of God along. "It is no light thing for any people in any age in the world to have a dispensation of the Gospel of Jesus Christ committed into their hands," said President Wilford Woodruff, "and when a dispensation has been given, those receiving it *are held responsible before high heaven for the use they make of it*" (*Journal of Discourses,* 22:205; italics added).

President Brigham Young declared:

> The powers of earth and hell have striven to destroy this kingdom from the earth. The wicked have succeeded in doing so in former ages; but this kingdom they cannot destroy, because it is the last dispensation—because it is the fulness of times. It is the dispensation of all dispensations and will excel in magnificence and glory every dispensation that has ever been committed to the children of men upon this earth. The Lord will bring again Zion, redeem his Israel, . . . and establish the laws of His Kingdom, and those laws will prevail. (*Journal of Discourses,* 8:36)

President Young gave this sober warning to the members of the Church:

> There is one principle I would like to have the Latter-day Saints perfectly understand—that is, of blessings and cursings. For instance, we read that war, pestilence, plagues, famine, etc., will be visited upon the inhabitants of the earth; but if distress through the judgments of God comes upon this people, it will be because the majority have turned away from the Lord. Let the majority of the people turn away from the Holy Commandments which the Lord has delivered to us, and cease to hold the balance of power in the Church, and we may expect the judgments of God to come upon us; but while *six-tenths, or three-fourths of this people will keep the commandments of God,* the curse and judgments of the Almighty will never come upon them, though we will have trials of various kinds, and the elements to contend with—natural and

spiritual elements. While this people will strive to serve God according to the best of their abilities, they will fare better, have more to eat and to wear, have better homes to live in, better associations, and enjoy themselves better than the wicked ever do or ever will do. (*Journal of Discourses* 10:335–36; italics added)

Apparently, as Latter-day Saints, we need a preponderance of our members to live the gospel and honor their covenants if we are to be protected from the judgments that will come with certainty unless the inhabitants of the land repent. But consider our present levels of activity and Church participation. What areas of Church activity function at a minimum level of "six-tenths, or three-fourths"—60 to 75 percent? How are we doing with respect to tithe payers? Young men on missions? Family home evenings? Temple marriages? If we are not reaching these performance levels, we cannot build Zion any more than could the earlier members of the Church. The Lord's rebuke still holds: "Those who call themselves after my name might be chastened for a little season with a sore and grievous chastisement, because they did not hearken altogether unto the precepts and commandments which I gave unto them" (D&C 103:4).

How are we doing in building stable marriages, avoiding the curse of divorce, stamping out pornography, and changing the media's efforts to exploit people by presenting sexual themes that lead to so much heartache and misery? We still must answer the question: Are we avoiding the negative elements of the Gentile culture, or are we embracing them and partaking of the sins of our day in an effort to be popular and to fit in to their society?

Every Member a Missionary

In the Doctrine and Covenants, the Lord counsels Church members to share the gospel with the Gentiles: "I sent you out to testify and warn the people, and it becometh every man who hath been warned to warn his neighbor. Therefore, they are left without excuse, and their sins are upon their own heads" (D&C 88:81–82).

Elder David B. Haight testified:

> An inspired prophet, David O. McKay, expanded this fundamental principle in 1959 while at the Hyde Park chapel in London, England. He proclaimed these four simple words: "Every member a missionary."
>
> In 1974, another prophet, Spencer W. Kimball, broadened our vision as he encouraged us to serve more diligently by lengthening our stride.
>
> . . . President Ezra Taft Benson declared: "Missionary work—the preaching of the gospel—has been the major activity of the true Church of Christ whenever the gospel has been upon the earth." (*Improvement Era,* June 1970, p. 95.)
>
> Each of us has a sacred duty to personally assist the accomplishment of the mission of the Church in proclaiming the gospel of our Lord Jesus Christ, perfecting the Saints to receive the ordinances of the gospel, and the teaching of the doctrines of salvation and the temple. ("Call to Serve," 83)

As Latter-day Saints, we must be about the significant mission given us because we possess the gospel and priesthood keys committed to the earth for the last time, in the last dispensation, for the blessing of our own families and for all of Heavenly Father's children.

Our faith and declaration is that this Church is the only true church upon the face of the earth (D&C 1:30). That claim may be offensive to some, no doubt, in a day of liberal theology and a lack of doctrinal emphasis. But we have been commissioned, and this work will proceed to its final culmination if we will do our part.

The Gentile Culture

A disturbing trend in the land in our day pertains to the right to express ourselves as Christians. Ironically, Christmas, a federal holiday honoring Christ, is now almost off-limits to Christians. "Merry Christmas" is now "Happy Holidays." We no longer have Christmas trees but rather "holiday trees." The message seems to be: "Spend money to help the economy, but don't pay attention to the message of Christ while you are shopping." This concern was mentioned by the First Presidency in 1979, and it has now grown to be a major issue:

> The Church . . . recognizes that a vital cornerstone of a free society is the principle of religious liberty. . . .
>
> We, thus, deplore the growing efforts to establish irreligion, such as atheism or secularism, as the official position of the United States of America, thus obscuring and eroding the rich and diverse religious heritage of our nation. We refer here to attacks on time-honored religious symbols in our public life. Such symbols include:
>
> 1. The reference to "one nation under God" in our pledge of allegiance;
>
> 2. The motto "In God We Trust" on our coins and public buildings;
>
> 3. "Praise [for] the power that hath made and preserved us a nation" in our national anthem;
>
> 4. Use of the Bible to administer official oaths;
>
> 5. The words "God Save the United States and this Honorable Court," spoken at the convening of the United States Supreme Court;
>
> 6. Prayers at the beginning of legislative sessions and other public meetings;
>
> 7. The performance of music with a religious origin or message in public programs;

8. The singing of Christmas carols and the location of nativity scenes or other seasonal decorations on public property during the Christmas holidays; and

9. References to God in public proclamations such as at Thanksgiving.

Those who oppose all references to God in our public life have set themselves the task of rooting out historical facts and ceremonial tributes and symbols so ingrained in our national consciousness that their elimination could only be interpreted as an official act of hostility toward religion. Our constitutional law forbids that. As the Supreme Court said in another leading case: "The place of religion in our society is an exalted one, achieved through a long tradition of reliance on the home, the church and the inviolable citadel of the individual heart and mind. We have come to recognize through bitter experience that it is not within the power of government to invade that citadel, whether its purpose or effect be to aid or oppose, to advance or retard. In the relationship between man and religion, the State is firmly committed to a position of neutrality (School District of Abington v. Schempp; 374 U.S. 203, 226 [1963]). ("News of the Church," 108–9)

That was more than a quarter of a century ago! Can anyone legitimately argue that the public display of the Ten Commandments establishes a state religion? Does public prayer or acknowledging God constitute an offense to the principles outlined in the Constitution? Do nativity scenes go against the principles of sound government? Some in our land would reduce Christmas to a secular event limited to Santa Claus, reindeer, elves, and shopping bags! Organizations immediately bring legal action if a religious practice or display appears in the public domain. On the other hand, alternative lifestyles that destroy the moral fabric of the country are considered free speech and defended in the courts of the land. Conservative values are ridiculed. Movies and other media portray individuals with religious values and beliefs as bordering on mentally unstable! More and more frequently, television and movies present morality as old-fashioned while murder, violence, and sexual promiscuity take front stage.

The Present and Future of America

We have entered a new millennium. We have enjoyed a period of relative peace and prosperity of unprecedented length in our nation during the past three decades. Though war is with us at present, we have had sufficient time to lay the foundation to carry out the three-fold mission of the Church. Perhaps we have become complacent. The Lord warned:

> Wherefore the decree hath gone forth from the Father that they shall be gathered in unto one place upon the face of this land, to prepare their hearts and be prepared in all things against the day when tribulation and desolation are sent forth upon the wicked.
>
> For the hour is nigh and the day soon at hand when the earth is ripe; and all the proud and they that do wickedly shall be as stubble; and I will burn them up, saith the Lord of Hosts, that wickedness shall not be upon the earth." (D&C 29:8–9)

> And thus, with the sword and by bloodshed the inhabitants of the earth shall mourn; and with famine, and plague, and earthquake, and the thunder of heaven, and the fierce and vivid lightning also, shall the inhabitants of the earth be made to feel the wrath, and indignation, and chastening hand of an Almighty God, until the consumption decreed hath made a full end of all nations. (D&C 87:6)

It appears that we are not going to sail off into the sunset.

Persecution may yet rear its ugly head again as the values and standards of the Church run counter to the immoral practices of the Gentiles. Latter-day Saints are required to make a difference in their communities. If there was ever a day in which Latter-day Saints could sit idly by and watch the ripening process take place, that day is past. We are moving into times that will try the hearts and souls of God's people.

Which Way Will the Gentiles Choose?

So, what does the future portend? Will the Gentiles accept the gospel of Jesus Christ as Church members and missionaries share their testimonies, or will the present inhabitants of the promised land become more and more entrenched in filth and debauchery? The answer is foreshadowed in a revelation given to Joseph Smith, in Doctrine and Covenants 45. The Lord reviewed some of the signs that would take place in the last days:

> And in that day shall be heard of wars and rumors of wars and the whole earth shall be in commotion, and men's hearts shall fail them, and they shall say that Christ delayeth his coming until the end of the earth.
>
> And the love of men shall wax cold, and iniquity shall abound.
>
> And when the times of the Gentiles is come in, a light shall break forth among them that sit in darkness, and it shall be the fulness of my gospel. (D&C 45:26–28)

After explaining the restoration of the gospel in the days of the Gentiles, the Lord said:

> But they receive it not; for they perceive not the light, and they turn their hearts from me because of the precepts of men.

And in that generation shall the times of the Gentiles be fulfilled.

And there shall be men standing in that generation, that shall not pass until they shall see an overflowing scourge; for a desolating sickness shall cover the land.

But my disciples shall stand in holy places, and shall not be moved; but among the wicked, men shall lift up their voices and curse God and die.

And there shall be earthquakes also in divers places, and many desolations; yet men will harden their hearts against me, and they will take up the sword, one against another, and they will kill one another. (D&C 45:29–33; italics added)

These revelations indicate that the Gentiles will not, in large numbers, accept the gospel. Nephi indicated the same thing: "Wo be unto the Gentiles, saith the Lord God of Hosts! For notwithstanding I shall lengthen out mine arm unto them from day to day, *they will deny me.*" He left the door open, however, if they would change: "Nevertheless, I will be merciful unto them, saith the Lord God, *if they will repent and come unto me;* for mine arm is lengthened out all the day long" (2 Nephi 28:32; italics added).

Such an ominous message should give Latter-day Saints the incentive to share the gospel with everyone with whom they come in contact. Sharing the message of the Book of Mormon is an important step in stopping the onward march of wickedness in this land. As the world ripens in further iniquity, the lives of the Saints must stand out as models for others to emulate, to be motivated to learn why the Latter-day Saints can be at peace in the midst of evil and social misery. Promises are extended to the faithful concerning divine protection if we are worthy of such blessings. The Lord explained to Joseph Smith about the days ahead:

And it shall be called the New Jerusalem, a land of peace, a city of refuge, a place of safety for the saints of the Most High God;

And the glory of the Lord shall be there, and the terror of the Lord also shall be there, insomuch that the wicked will not come unto it, and it shall be called Zion.

And it shall come to pass among the wicked, that every man that will not take his sword against his neighbor must needs flee unto Zion for safety.

And there shall be gathered unto it out of every nation under heaven; and it shall be the only people that shall not be at war one with another.

And it shall be said among the wicked: Let us not go up to battle against Zion, for the inhabitants of Zion are terrible; wherefore we cannot stand.

And it shall come to pass that the righteous shall be gathered out from among all nations, and shall come to Zion, singing with songs of everlasting joy. (D&C 45:66–71)

The revelation concludes: "And all nations shall be afraid because of the terror of the Lord, and the power of his might. Even so. Amen" (D&C 45:75).

It appears that the stages of decline will continue. Days of persecution apparently lie ahead. From the verses quoted above, however, we know that the Lord is in control, and He has the power to protect the Saints if need be—but only if we are giving Him our best efforts. If we are faithfully carrying out our mission, He has promised that He will "preserve the righteous by his power, even if it so be that the fulness of his wrath must come, and the righteous be preserved, even unto the destruction of their enemies by fire. Wherefore, the righteous need not fear; for thus saith the prophet, they shall be saved, even if it so be as by fire" (1 Nephi 22:17).

The scriptures contain positive promises to the righteous. Presently, we live in a day of quiet optimism and opportunity to bless the Gentiles. Never has there been a better time to live on the earth. But it is also a day of vigilance, of warning, of heeding the word of the Lord, and of listening carefully to the counsel of prophets. Dangers lurk in the world, as 9/11 demonstrated. We must learn from the Jaredites what happens when people fail to heed prophetic counsel. When people become complacent and caught up in their own selfish interests, when they neglect family and neighbors, when they break covenants and family ties, the Spirit of the Lord withdraws, and they are left to suffer the results of their own pride and wickedness.

Our task is to show the Gentiles a better way and appeal to them in sufficient numbers to prevent the judgments of God from coming upon this land until we have given them every opportunity to partake. But in the long run, it appears that another Jaredite, Nephite, and Antediluvian tragedy is in the making. The Lord may have to intervene to rescue the righteous as He did in the past. This time, perhaps, it will be by His coming to usher in the Millennium, a thousand years of peace, when war will be no more, when the prophecies and the great work of that period will be fulfilled. Mortals do not know how far away that time period may be.

The signs of the times are clearly upon us. As the Saints of God, we must rise to our tallest spiritual stature as missionaries, emissaries, and models of right and decent living if we are to influence this nation to avoid the tragedies that took down previous civilizations on the land. Latter-day Saints can make a difference. We must make a difference. We now have sufficient numbers to affect for good the nations of the earth. That influence can only increase if we will be true to our covenants, to our way of life, to the God of heaven. He is depending on us to save the rest of His family, if they will receive His gospel. The simple key for Latter-day Saints is to follow the prophets, seers, and revelators who teach us the way to salvation. The events of the future will test the souls of the Saints. Exciting and thrilling days lie ahead as the hand of God is made manifest in the affairs of men.

Listen again to the warnings of the last two authors of the Book of Mormon record to us and the Gentiles of our day:

> Turn, all ye Gentiles from your wicked ways; and repent of your evil doings, of your lyings and deceivings, and of your whoredoms, and of your secret abominations, and your idolatries, and of your murders, and your priestcrafts, and your envyings, and your strifes, and from all your wickedness and abominations, and come unto me, and be baptized in my name, that ye may receive a remission of your sins, and be filled with the Holy Ghost, that ye may be numbered with my people who are of the house of Israel. (3 Nephi 30:2)

And Moroni's plea rings in our ears:

> This cometh unto you, O ye Gentiles, that ye may know the decrees of God—that ye may repent, and not continue in your iniquities until the fulness come, that ye may not bring down the fulness of the wrath of God upon you as the inhabitants of the land have hitherto done.
>
> Behold, this is a choice land, and whatsoever nation shall possess it shall be free from bondage, and from captivity, and from all other nations under heaven, if they will but serve the God of the land, who is Jesus Christ, who hath been manifested by the things which we have written. (Ether 2:11–12)

Elder Gordon B. Hinckley, years ago, gave this warning, which still applies:

> The word of the Lord is clear that those who do not keep the commandments and observe the laws of God shall be burned at the time of his coming. For that shall be a day of

judgment and a day of sifting, a day of separating the good from the evil. . . .

It will be a time of great and terrible fears, of cataclysmic upheavals of nature, of weeping and wailing, of repentance too late, and of crying out unto the Lord for mercy. But for those who in that judgment are found acceptable, it will be a day for thanksgiving, for the Lord shall come with his angels, and the apostles who were with him in Jerusalem, and those who have been resurrected. Further, the graves of the righteous will be opened and they shall come forth. Then will begin the great Millennium, a period of a thousand years when Satan shall be bound and the Lord shall reign over his people. Can you imagine the wonder and the beauty of that era when the adversary shall not have influence? Think of his pull upon you now and reflect on the peace of that time when you will be free from such influence. There will be quiet and goodness where now there is contention and evil. . . .

Certainly there is no point in speculating concerning the day and the hour. Let us rather live each day so that if the Lord does come while we are yet upon the earth we shall be worthy of that change which will occur as in the twinkling of an eye and under which we shall be changed from mortal to immortal beings. And if we should die before he comes then—if our lives have conformed to his teachings—we shall arise in that resurrection morning and be partakers of the marvelous experiences designed for those who shall live and work with the Savior in that promised Millennium. We need not fear the day of his coming; the very purpose of the Church is to provide the incentive and the opportunity for us to conduct our lives in such a way that those who are members of the kingdom of God will become members of the kingdom of heaven when he establishes that kingdom on the earth. ("We Need Not Fear His Coming," 82–83)

14

America's Hope

At first glance, the future of this land might seem a little worrisome. Any fair observer who looks at the wickedness and perversions that exist among the Gentiles would not be optimistic that things will change for the better in the coming years. We might ask: Is the music of the future going to become more refined? Are the movies coming out of Hollywood going to become more conservative? Will television programs return to positive themes concerning morality and marriage and family life? Hardly. The extent of evil and violence is widespread and seems to be increasing in intensity. It appears that there is little incentive for media executives to choose to depict themes that honor honesty, integrity, marriage, and family values in harmony with our Creator. As President Boyd K. Packer observed:

> The world is spiraling downward at an ever-quickening pace.
> I am sorry to tell you that it will not get better. . . .
>
> I know of nothing in the history of the Church or in the history of the world to compare with our present circumstances.

Nothing happened in Sodom and Gomorrah which exceeds in wickedness and depravity that which surrounds us now.

Words of profanity, vulgarity, and blasphemy are heard everywhere. Unspeakable wickedness, perversion, and abuse were once hidden in dark places; now they are in the open, even accorded legal protection.

At Sodom and Gomorrah these things were localized. Now they are spread across the world, and they are among us. . . .

. . . Satan uses every intrigue to disrupt the family.

The sacred relationship between man and woman, husband and wife, through which mortal bodies are conceived and life is passed from one generation to the next generation, is being showered with filth.

Surely you can see what the adversary is about. The first line of defense, the home, is crumbling. ("One Pure Defense," 4)

A glance at our nation at present shows a country fighting terrorism, pervasive immorality and adultery on every screen, Sabbathbreaking at new levels as college sports are played out on Sunday, an increasing acceptance of cohabitation, out-of-wedlock immorality, abuse of child, spouse, and the elderly, fatherless homes, homosexual behavior, same gender advocates pleading for the marriage label, abortion, loss of religious influence in the public domain, pornography, divorce, rebellious children, filthy movies, sleazy videos, Internet misuse, false religious concepts, unemployment and economic challenges, and loss of hope, just to name a few.

The Hope

With such a dismal outlook, hope, if there is to be any, must come from prophets, who see things ahead of us that are not apparent from the daily news channels. It is the responsibility of prophets to speak for God, to help us see our way out of the present distress

(D&C 21:4–6). God preserved this nation in the past: Patriots shed blood, which nourished the soil on which this country became the city on the hill. It is to prophets that the righteous look for the hope of a brighter day, perhaps even for divine intervention.

There are precedents for the Lord stepping in to preserve His Saints when the forces of evil were overwhelming: Moses taking Israel through the Red Sea; David and Goliath; Isaiah telling Hezekiah the Assyrian army camped at Jerusalem's gates would do no harm; Daniel surviving the lion's den; Shadrach, Meshach, and Abed-nego in Babylon; Elisha's statement to his servant: "Fear not: for they that be with us are more than they that be with them" (2 Kings 6:16). Divine intervention came in the form of a Liahona to Lehi, of ship-building instruction to Nephi, an angel's appearing to Alma the Younger, of prison walls falling down around the brothers Nephi and Lehi. Intervention came as a young boy's prayer was answered at a time when the religious world was compounding ignorance about the nature of God and the plan of salvation. In that marvelous reve-lation, the heavens opened, and a way out of the hopeless morass of religious confusion and distorted doctrines brought a fresh renewal of the gospel of Jesus Christ. Hope came to the pioneers in the form of seagulls as marauding crickets were destroying their crops.

The point is that God ever rules in the heavens; He is the God of the universe. He has all power, and if His children obey His com-mandments and live the gospel despite living in a world of evil, divine intervention is not out of the realm of possibility. From the way the Gentiles are desecrating Christ and His teachings and Christian principles in general, it appears that the Lord may have to intervene to preserve His people in the coming days. If such miracles are to take place, the Lord will make them known to his prophets (Amos 3:8).

The sermons of recent presidents of the Church project an opti-mism that can only come through inspiration and revelation. But even in that optimism, their messages assume that the Latter-day Saints will do their part. There is no time for complacency (2 Nephi 28:14, 21).

What have recent prophets said concerning the future of this nation? Examples from the teachings of the past five Church presidents indicate their thoughts and insights about the coming days.

President Harold B. Lee

In a classic address given in 1973 at Ricks College (now BYU–Idaho), President Harold B. Lee said:

> We are living in a time of great crisis. The country is torn with scandal and with criticism, with faultfinding and condemnation. There are those who have downgraded the image of this nation as probably never before in the history of the country. It is so easy to clamber onto the bandwagon and to join the extremists in condemnation, little realizing that when they commit their actions, they are not just tearing down a man; they are tearing down a nation, and they are striking at the underpinnings of one of the greatest of all the nations of all the world— a nation that was founded upon an inspired declaration we call the Constitution of the United States. The Lord said it was written by men whom He raised up for that very purpose, and that Constitution stands today as a model to all nations to pattern their lives. . . .
>
> Some time ago the First Presidency and the Council of the Twelve were engaged in a meeting of serious import, and I said something at that time unpremeditated, but I couldn't have said it better had I taken a month to prepare it. I said:
>
> " . . . I think we must be on the optimistic side. This is a great nation; this is a great country; this is the most favored of all lands. While it is true that there are dangers and difficulties

that lie ahead of us, we must not assume that we are going to stand by and watch the country go to ruin. We should not be heard to predict ills and calamities for the nation. On the contrary, we should be providing optimistic support for the nation.

"You must remember, brethren, that this church is one of the most powerful agencies for the progress of the world, and we should all bear our testimonies that we must all sound with one voice. We must tell the world how we feel about this land and this nation and should bear our testimonies about the great mission and destiny that it has. These are the subjects we should be talking about, brethren, and if we do this, we will help turn the tide of this great country and lessen the influence of the pessimists. We must be careful that we do not say or do anything that will further weaken the country. It is the negative, pessimistic comments about the nation that do as much harm as anything to the country today. We who carry these sacred responsibilities must preach the gospel of peace, and peace can only come by overcoming the things of the world. Now, we must be the dynamic force that will help turn the tide of fear and pessimism. . . .

"I think our people are just waiting for somebody to tell them the way to go. Our people are like soldiers in the ranks. They are waiting for us as leaders to tell them which way to go, and brethren, we must tell them in a positive way what they should be doing. This is the Lord's way, and so we should not be concerned about finding out what is wrong with America, but we should be finding what is right about America and should be speaking optimistically and enthusiastically about America." (*Ye Are the Light of the World*, 340–42)

In this same address, President Lee discussed the pessimism that gripped many of the citizens before the Revolutionary War when it seemed fruitless to fight against the power of Great Britain. He reviewed how the Civil War threatened the end of the United States as it appeared that a division was all but certain. He recalled how at the death of Joseph and Hyrum Smith many thought Mormonism would end. He pointed out that sometimes people respond better during periods of testing than at any other time, and he quoted Helaman 12:2–5, pleading for the Latter-day Saints to not become proud or arrogant in spite of economic prosperity. Then he spoke of this nation's future:

> Men may fail in this country, earthquakes may come, seas may heave beyond their bounds, there may be great drought, disaster, and hardship, but this nation, founded on principles laid down by men whom God raised up, will never fail. This is the cradle of humanity, where life on this earth began in the Garden of Eden. This is the place of the new Jerusalem. This is the place that the Lord said is favored above all other nations in all the world. This is the place where the Savior will come to His temple. This is the favored land in all the world. Yes, I repeat, men may fail, but this nation won't fail. I have faith in America; you and I must have faith in America, if we understand the teachings of the gospel of Jesus Christ. We are living in a day when we *must* pay heed to these challenges.
>
> I plead with you not to preach pessimism. Preach that this is the greatest country in all the world. This is the favored land. This is the land of our forefathers. It is the nation that will stand despite whatever trials or crises it may yet have to pass through.
>
> The Lord will not leave His church without direction. Revelation for our guidance comes to the leadership of the kingdom of God on earth. (*Ye Are the Light of the World,* 350–51)

President Spencer W. Kimball

President Spencer W. Kimball applied Daniel's interpretation of Nebuchadnezzar's dream to this land:

This is a revelation concerning the history of the world, when one world power would supersede another until there would be numerous smaller kingdoms to share the control of the earth.

And it was in the days of these kings that power would not be given to men, but the God of heaven would set up a kingdom—the kingdom of God upon the earth, which should never be destroyed nor left to other people.

The Church of Jesus Christ of Latter-day Saints was restored in 1830 after numerous revelations from the divine source; and this is the kingdom, set up by the God of heaven, that would never be destroyed nor superseded, and the stone cut out of the mountain without hands that would become a great mountain and would fill the whole earth. ("Stone Cut without Hands," 8–9)

President Ezra Taft Benson

President Ezra Taft Benson pleaded with the Saints to carefully read the Book of Mormon, and he had much to say about this nation and its future: "It may cost us blood before we are through. It is my conviction, however, that when the Lord comes, the Stars and Stripes will be floating on the breeze over this people" (*Teachings of Ezra Taft Benson,* 618).

In the following statement, he addressed the options that face the Gentiles and Latter-day Saints:

The Lord told the Prophet Joseph Smith there would be an attempt to overthrow the country by destroying the Constitution. Joseph Smith predicted that the time would come when the Constitution would hang, as it were, by a thread, and at that time "this people will step forth and save it from the threatened destruction" (*Journal of Discourses,* 7:15).

It is my conviction that the elders of Israel, widely spread over the nation, will at that crucial time successfully rally the righteous of our country and provide the necessary balance of strength to save the institutions of constitutional government.

If the Gentiles on this land reject the word of God and conspire to overthrow liberty and the Constitution, their doom is fixed, and they "shall be cut off from among my people who are of the covenant" (1 Nephi 14:6; 3 Nephi 21:11, 14, 21; D&C 84:114–15, 117). (*Teachings of Ezra Taft Benson,* 618–19)

When this nation was established, the Church was restored and from here the message of the restored gospel has gone forth—all according to divine plan. This then becomes the Lord's base of operations in these latter days. And this base— the land of America—will not be shifted out of its place. This nation will, in a measure at least, fulfill its mission even though it may face serious and troublesome days. The degree to which it achieves its full mission *depends upon the righteousness of its people.* God, through His power, has established a free people in this land as a means of helping to carry forward His purposes.

It was His latter-day purpose to bring forth His gospel in America, not in any other place. It was in America where the Book of Mormon plates were deposited. That was no accident. It was His design. It was in this same America where they were brought to light by angelic ministry. . . . It was here where He organized His modern Church, where He, Himself, made a modern personal appearance (see D&C 20:1; Joseph Smith–History 1:17).

It was here under a free government and a strong nation that protection was provided for His restored Church. Now God will not permit America, His base of operations, to be destroyed. He has promised protection to this land if we will but serve the God of the land (see Ether 2:12). He has also promised protection to the righteous even, if necessary, to send fire from heaven to destroy their enemies (1 Nephi 22:17).

No, God's base of operations will not be destroyed. But it may be weakened and made less effective. One of the first rules of war strategy—and we are at war with the adversary and his agents—is to protect the base of operations. This we must do if we are to build up the kingdom throughout the world and safeguard our God-given freedom.

We must protect this base of operations from every threat— from sin, from unrighteousness, from immorality, from desecration of the Sabbath day, from lawlessness, from parental and juvenile delinquency. We must protect it from dirty movies, from filthy advertising, from salacious and suggestive television programs, magazines, and books.

We must protect this base from idleness, subsidies, doles, and soft governmental paternalism which weakens initiative, discourages industry, destroys character, and demoralizes the people.

To protect this base we must protect the soul of America— we must return to a love and respect for the basic spiritual concepts upon which this nation has been established. We must study the Constitution and the writings of the Founding Fathers. (*Teachings of Ezra Taft Benson,* 571–72; italics added)

President Howard W. Hunter

President Howard W. Hunter was not pleased with negative and discouraging comments and attitudes of some citizens of this land:

I am here tonight to tell you that despair, doom, and discouragement are not an acceptable view of life for a Latter-day Saints. However high on the charts they are on the hit parade of contemporary news, we must not walk on our lower lip every time a few difficult moments happen to confront us. (*Teachings of Howard W. Hunter,* 199)

Here are some actual comments that have been made and passed on to me in recent months. This comes from a fine returned missionary:

Why should I date and get serious with a girl? I am not sure I even want to marry and bring a family into this kind of a world. I am not very sure about my own future. How can I take the responsibility for the future of others whom I would love and care about and want to be happy?

Here's another from a high school student:

I hope I die before all these terrible things happen that people are talking about. I don't want to be on the earth when there is so much trouble.

And this from a recent college graduate:

I am doing the best I can, but I wonder if there is much reason to even plan for the future, let alone retirement. The world probably won't last that long anyway.

Well, isn't that a fine view of things. Sounds like we all ought to go and eat a big plate of worms.

I want to say to all within the sound of my voice tonight that you have every reason in this world to be happy and to be optimistic and to be confident. Every generation since time began has had some things to overcome and some problems to work out. Furthermore, every individual person has a particular set of challenges that sometimes seems to be earmarked for us individually. We understood that in our premortal existence. (*Teachings of Howard W. Hunter,* 199–200)

I promise you tonight in the name of the Lord whose servant I am that God will always protect and care for his people. We will have our difficulties the way every generation and people have had difficulties. . . . But with the gospel of Jesus Christ you have every hope and promise and reassurance. The

Lord has power over his Saints and will always prepare places of peace, defense, and safety for his people. When we have faith in God we can hope for a better world—for us personally and for all mankind. . . .

Disciples of Christ in every generation are invited, indeed commanded, to be filled with a perfect brightness of hope (2 Nephi 31:20). (*Teachings of Howard W. Hunter*, 201)

I am frank to say tonight that I hope you won't believe all the world's difficulties have been wedged into your decade or that things have never been worse than they are for you personally, or that they will never get better. I reassure you that things have been worse and they *will* always get better. They always do—especially when we live and love the gospel of Jesus Christ and give it a chance in our lives. (*Teachings of Howard W. Hunter*, 202)

President Gordon B. Hinckley

President Gordon B. Hinckley, God's prophet for more than a decade now, has been especially optimistic about the progress and future of the Church and its impact on the world community. Reading his words instills optimism in the hearts of the faithful and impels them to greater patriotism. His messages remind us that God will not allow the righteous to be destroyed, even if it becomes necessary for Him to intervene. Following are some of President Hinckley's statements from recent years. He said in the October general conference of 1997:

Something, my brothers and sisters, is happening in this Church, something wonderful. As we walk in the small world of our individual wards and branches we are scarcely aware of it. And yet it is real, and it is tremendous. We are growing. We are expanding. Enough people will come into the Church this year to constitute more than 600 new wards or branches. . . .

We were recently with the Navajo Nation at Window Rock in Arizona. It was the first time that a President of the Church had met with and spoken to them in their capital. It was difficult to hold back the tears as we mingled with these sons and daughters of Father Lehi. In my imagination I have seen him weeping for his progeny who for so long have walked in poverty and pain.

But the shackles of darkness are falling. Some of them now are men and women of achievement. They have partaken of the fruits of education. They have come to know and love the gospel. They have become pure and delightsome.

But there is so much more to do among them. . . .

We have been with thousands of these wonderful people in South America. . . .

We have now been in all the nations of South America and Central America, and we have seen miracles, with great gatherings of 30,000, 40,000, and 50,000 in football stadiums. These are all Latter-day Saints. In each case as we left there was a great waving of handkerchiefs, with tears in their eyes and tears in ours.

In the nation of Brazil alone there will be approximately 50,000 people join the Church this year. That is the equivalent of 16 or 17 new stakes in just 12 months. The São Paulo Temple cannot accommodate all who wish to come. We are building three new temples in that nation and will yet have to build others.

These are strong and wonderful Latter-day Saints in whose hearts beat the same testimonies of Jesus and this work as beat in yours.

We must construct meetinghouses by the score to accommodate the needs of these ever-increasing numbers.

I stand in amazement, knowing the history of this Church, when I realize there is not a city in the United States or Canada of any consequence which does not have a Latter-day Saint congregation. It is the same in Mexico. It is the same in Central and South America. Likewise in New Zealand and Australia, in the islands of the sea, and in Japan, Korea, Taiwan, the Philippines.

In Europe our congregations are everywhere. What a remarkable thing it is to contemplate that each Sabbath there are more than 24,000 wards and branches across the world in which the same lessons are taught and the same testimonies are borne.

Now, what of the future? What of the years that lie ahead? *It looks promising indeed.* People are beginning to see us for what we are and for the values we espouse. The media generally treat us well. We enjoy a good reputation, for which we are grateful.

If we will go forward, never losing sight of our goal, speaking ill of no one, living the great principles we know to be true, *this cause will roll on in majesty and power to fill the earth. Doors now closed to the preaching of the gospel will be opened. The Almighty, if necessary, may have to shake the nations to humble them and cause them to listen to the servants of the living God. Whatever is needed will come to pass.*

The great challenges facing us and the key to the success of the work *will be the faith of all who call themselves Latter-day Saints.* Our standards are certain and unequivocal. We need not quibble about them. We need not rationalize them. They are set forth in the Decalogue written by the finger of the Lord on Mount Sinai. They are found in the Sermon on the Mount spoken by the Lord Himself. They are found elsewhere in His teachings, and they are found plainly set forth in the words of modern revelation. From the beginning these have served as our code of conduct. They must continue to so serve.

The future will be essentially the same as the past, *only much brighter and greatly enlarged.* We must continue to reach out across the world, teaching the gospel at home and abroad. A divine mandate rests heavily upon us. We cannot run from it. We cannot avoid it. . . .

There must be *no diminution in our effort to carry the gospel to the people of the earth.* In the future even more of our young men must prepare themselves to go out in service to the Lord. Our Christian acts must precede them and accompany them wherever necessary. I am grateful for the humanitarian aid we have been able to extend to the poor and the unfortunate. . . .

As we look to the future we must extend the great work carried forward in the temples, both for the living and the dead. If this people cannot be saved without their dead, as the Prophet Joseph declared, then we must make it possible for many more to accomplish this work. . . .

But there are many other things we must do as we move forward the work to a new and promising century. *Simply put, we must be better Latter-day Saints.* We must be more neighborly. We cannot live a cloistered existence in this world. We are a part of the whole of humanity. . . .

I mention the Sabbath day. The Sabbath of the Lord is becoming the play day of the people. It is a day of golf and football on television, of buying and selling in our stores and markets. Are we moving to mainstream America as some observers believe? In this I fear we are. What a telling thing it is to see the parking lots of the markets filled on Sunday in communities that are predominately LDS.

Our strength for the future, our resolution to grow the Church across the world, will be weakened if we violate the will of the Lord in this important matter. He has so very clearly spoken anciently and again in modern revelation. We cannot disregard with impunity that which He has said. . . . .

We must observe the Word of Wisdom. . . .

Now, in closing, I see a wonderful future in a very uncertain world. If we will cling to our values, if we will build on our inheritance, if we will walk in obedience before the Lord, if we will simply live the gospel we will be blessed in a magnificent and wonderful way. We will be looked upon as a peculiar people who have found the key to a peculiar happiness . . .

We have glimpsed the future, we know the way, we have the truth. God help us to move forward to become a great and mighty people spread over the earth, counted in the millions, but all of one faith and of one testimony and of one conviction. ("Look to the Future," 67–69; italics added)

In the October general conference of 2003, he commented:

There is never reason to despair. This is the work of God. Notwithstanding the efforts of all who oppose it, it will go forward as the God of heaven has designed it should do. . . .

I believe and testify that it is the mission of this Church to stand as an ensign to the nations and a light to the world. We have had placed upon us a great, all-encompassing mandate from which we cannot shrink nor turn aside. We accept that mandate and are determined to fulfill it, and with the help of God we shall do it.

There are forces all around us that would deter us from that effort. The world is constantly crowding in on us. From all sides we feel the pressure to soften our stance, to give in here a little and there a little. . . .

We must stand firm. We must hold back the world. If we do so, the Almighty will be our strength and our protector, our guide and our revelator. We shall have the comfort of knowing that we are doing what He would have us do. Others may not agree with us, but I am confident that they will respect us. We will not be left alone. There are many not of our faith but who feel as we do. They will support us. They will sustain us in our efforts. . . .

God bless you, my dear young friends. You are the best

generation we have ever had. You know the gospel better. You are more faithful in your duties. You are stronger to face the temptations which come your way. Live by your standards. Pray for the guidance and protection of the Lord. He will never leave you alone. He will comfort you. He will sustain you. He will bless and magnify you and make your reward sweet and beautiful. And you will discover that your example will attract others who will take courage from your strength.

As it is with the youth, so it is with you adults. If we are to hold up this Church as an ensign to the nations and a light to the world, we must take on more of the luster of the life of Christ individually and in our own personal circumstances. In standing for the right, we must not be fearful of the consequences. We must never be afraid. . . .

I remind all of us that we are Latter-day Saints. We have made covenants with our Heavenly Father, sacred and binding. Those covenants, if we keep them, will make us better fathers and mothers, better sons and daughters.

I believe that others will rally around us if we will do so. We can stand for truth and goodness, and we will not stand alone. *Moreover, we shall have the unseen forces of heaven to assist us. . . .*

The Lord has said to us:

"Therefore, fear not, little flock; do good; let earth and hell combine against you, for if ye are built upon my rock, *they cannot prevail.* ("Ensign to the Nations, a Light to the World," 82–85; italics added)

In an address in the April 2004 general conference, he gave this positive assessment:

Our times are fraught with peril. We hear frequently quoted the words of Paul to Timothy: "This know also, that in the last days perilous times shall come" (2 Timothy 3:1). He then goes on to describe the conditions that will prevail. I think it is plainly evident that these latter days are indeed perilous times that fit the conditions that Paul described (see 2 Timothy 3:2–7). . . .

And, my brothers and sisters, this places upon each of us a grand and consuming responsibility. President Wilford Woodruff said in 1894:

The Almighty is with this people. We shall have all the revelations that we will need, if we will do our duty and obey the commandments of God. . . . While I . . . live I want to do my duty. I want the Latter-day Saints to do their duty. Here is the Holy Priesthood. . . . Their responsibility is great and mighty. The eyes of God and all the holy prophets are watching us. This is the great dispensation that has been spoken of ever since the world began. We are gathered together . . . by the power and commandment of God. We are doing the work of God. . . . Let us fill our mission" (in James R. Clark, comp., *Messages of the First Presidency of The Church of Jesus Christ of Latter-day Saints,* 6 vols. [1965–75], 3:258).

This is our great and demanding challenge, my brothers and sisters. This is the choice we must constantly make, just as generations before us have had to choose. . . .

We must do all that is required in moving forward the work of the Lord in building His kingdom in the earth. We can never compromise the doctrine which has come through revelation, but we can live and work with others, respecting their beliefs and admiring their virtues, joining hands in opposition to the sophistries, the quarrels, the hatred—those perils which have been with man from the beginning.

Without surrendering any element of our doctrine, we can be neighborly, we can be helpful, we can be kind and generous.

We of this generation are the end harvest of all that has gone before. It is not enough to simply be known as a member of this Church. A solemn obligation rests upon us. Let us face it and work at it.

We must live as true followers of the Christ, with charity toward all, returning good for evil, teaching by example the ways of the Lord, and accomplishing the vast service He has outlined for us. ("Dawning of a Brighter Day," 81–84)

From this prophet's perspective it doesn't sound like the Church is going to fail. And if the Church is going to be here, then the country must be here.

Summary

When we read the words of the last five Church presidents, we don't get the idea that we ought to fold up our tents just now. They all are optimistic that if—*if*—the Latter-day Saints will live the gospel and keep their baptismal and temple covenants, share the gospel, and continue to serve in His Church, pay their tithing, and attend to the three-fold mission of the Church, the future indeed looks bright.

Perhaps we could summarize the reasons why this nation will survive despite the challenges that seem almost insurmountable at the present time:

1. *New Jerusalem.* Ancient prophets have seen on this land the New Jerusalem that is yet in the future (Ether 13:3–10).

2. *The United States of America.* This nation was created by the hand of God. Its Constitution was created by "wise men whom I raised up unto this very purpose" (D&C 101:80), and there will be sufficient numbers of righteous people who will support the major provisions of this inspired instrument of government.

3. *Large number of Latter-day Saints.* Never have there been as many members on the earth in this dispensation as there are now. If the Saints can avoid the trappings of the adversary, if they will do their best, God will honor them by preserving them even in the midst of great evil on this planet.

4. *The final dispensation.* The Lord's Church was restored here. This land is sacred. The final dispensation began in this land with the calling of Joseph Smith, the latter-day prophet. The Lord will protect this nation, the cradle of the Restoration, if the Saints will keep their covenants. This final dispensation cannot and will not end in defeat.

5. *The Book of Mormon.* The Book of Mormon was preserved to come forth in this land to restore the basic principles and doctrines of the gospel of Jesus Christ. It "contains a record of a fallen people, and the fulness of the gospel of Jesus Christ to the Gentiles and to the Jews also; . . . proving to the world that the holy scriptures are true, and that God does inspire men and call them to his holy work in this age and generation, as well as in generations of old" (D&C 20:9–11).

6. *Ancient prophets.* Prophets of old, perhaps discouraged with events in their own day, looked to our day with "anxious expectation" (D&C 121:27; see also vv. 26, 28–29). They saw the founding of this nation. They knew that the dispensation that would begin here would pave the way for the second coming of Jesus Christ to usher in the Millennium.

7. *God's promise of protection to the righteous.* God will protect the righteous even if it requires divine intervention. This promise has always been a part of the covenant between God and those who abide on this land (Ether 2:7–12; 2 Nephi 1:1–4, 9; 1 Nephi 14:1–2, 6). We now have a large number of faithful people in the Church, and many honest people outside the Church will yet join with us to preserve a righteous lifestyle.

8. *The youth of the Church.* Because of teachings they receive in the home, in seminary and institute, and through serving missions, the youth will stay true to the commandments, marry in the temple, and serve in the kingdom of God on earth. This is true of young members of the Church in this nation, which is the Lord's base of operations, and in the world.

9. *Temple building and temple work.* In family history research, Church members are usually unable to trace family members beyond the sixteenth or seventeenth century. The Millennium will be a time of temple activity, and those who have been in the spirit realm for centuries will reveal to those on the earth what ordinances must be performed. Elder Dallin H. Oaks said: "Many of the most important deprivations of mortality will be set right in the Millennium, which is the time for fulfilling all that is incomplete in the great plan of happiness for all of our Father's worthy children. We know that will be true of temple ordinances. I believe it will also be true of family relationships and experiences" ("Great Plan of Happiness," 75).

It is the Latter-day Saints who must build the temples in which ordinances can be performed for all of the righteous dead during the millennial era. Temple building continues in this nation and in the world.

10. *The promises of living prophets.* As we have seen, the past five Church presidents give no indication that this nation will be swept aside with the destruction of the Gentiles. Though there will be abundant worries, daunting trials, challenges to decency and right thinking, and great wickedness, the Saints, if they are faithful, will see the hand of the Lord in their lives and the lives of their leaders to a greater extent in the decades ahead.

Summary

This nation is to survive until the second coming of the Lord Jesus Christ, when the work of God will be consummated, when the king of heaven shall descend and put an end to all warfare, evil, and wickedness, and the great work of the Millennium will be underway. The bad news is that the ripening process will continue among the wicked; the good news is that the righteous will become even more committed to the work of God.

The possibility of good news appears to be grounded in "if" clauses. *If* the Latter-day Saints follow their prophets, *if* divine laws embodied in constitutional principles are upheld, *if* the Church's youth rise above the gross evils of immorality and continue to serve missions, *if* temples and temple work are used to redeem the dead, *if* the members of the Church live the principles of the gospel, share the message of the Restoration, marry in the temple, and so forth, then the judgments of God will be delayed (1 Nephi 22:17–20, 26), or the Saints will be preserved in the midst of the gathering evil. And *if* the honest in heart among the Gentiles, who fear God and understand biblical principles, respond to the message of the Restoration and join in the effort to restore decency among the people, there *is* hope for the future of our society. Latter-day Saints, obviously, have no small role to play in this winding-up scene. We must be models, individually and as families, to lead the Gentiles back to a state of goodness. We must light the way out of the present moral abyss and set this nation back on the path of righteousness. *If* this can be done in sufficient numbers, this nation will survive the severe tests and challenges that lie ahead.

A statement in the Wentworth letter by the first Prophet of this dispensation summarizes our future:

> No unhallowed hand can stop the work from progressing; persecutions may rage, mobs may combine, armies may assemble, calumny may defame, but the truth of God will go forth boldly, nobly, and independent, till it has penetrated every continent, visited every clime, swept every country, and sounded in every ear, till the purposes of God shall be accomplished, and the Great Jehovah shall say the work is done. (*History of the Church*, 4:540)

So be it!

Notes

CHAPTER 2

AMERICA, THE PROMISED LAND

1. Joseph Smith, in a Church conference in 1844, said that the whole of North and South America encompassed the land of Zion (*Teachings of the Prophet Joseph Smith,* 362). The earth land mass was in one piece at the time of the Creation, and it was later divided into continents in the days of Peleg (Genesis 10:25). Adam and Eve were placed in the Garden "eastward in Eden" (Moses 3:8) and after being cast out of the Garden lived in an area within what now known as the state of Missouri (see D&C 117:8). Elder James E. Talmage wrote that a revelation was "given through Joseph Smith, at Spring Hill, Mo., May 19, 1838, in which that place [Eden] is named by the Lord 'Adam-ondi-Ahman, because, said he, it is the place where Adam shall come to visit his people, or the Ancient of Days shall sit, as spoken of by Daniel the prophet' (D.& C. sec. 116). From another revelation we learn (D.&C. 107:52, 53) that three years before his death, Adam called together in the valley of Adam-ondi-Ahman those of his sons who had been made high priests, together with the rest of his righteous posterity, and there bestowed upon them his patriarchal blessings, the event being marked by special manifestations from the Lord (see also D.&C. 117:8)" (*Articles of Faith,* 474).

2. See *Book of Mormon Student Manual,* 136; see also Largey, *Book of Mormon Reference Companion,* 435.

3. Lehi stated that "there shall none come into this land save they shall be brought by the hand of the Lord." And further, "the Lord hath covenanted this land unto me, and to my children forever, and also *all those who should be led out of other countries by the hand of the Lord*" (2 Nephi 1:5–6; italics added). Initially, people from all nations and religions of the earth were led to this land in the final dispensation before the Millennium.

4. President Joseph Fielding Smith wrote: "In accord with the revelations given to the Prophet Joseph Smith, we teach that the Garden of Eden was on the American continent located where the City Zion, or the New Jerusalem, will be built. When Adam and Eve were driven out of the Garden, they eventually dwelt at a place called Adam-ondi-Ahman, situated in what is now Daviess County, Missouri. Three years before the death of Adam he called the righteous of his posterity at this place and blessed them, and it is at this place where Adam, or Michael, will sit as we read in the 7th chapter of Daniel. We are committed to the fact that Adam dwelt on this American continent. But when Adam dwelt here, it was not the American continent, nor was it the Western Hemisphere, for all the land was in one place, and all the water was in one place" (*Doctrines of Salvation,* 3:74).

5. Canada's highest court on December 2004 declared that marriage can be redefined by political leaders to include same-gender couples.

CHAPTER 3

AMERICA: PAST, PRESENT, AND FUTURE

1. Elder David B. Haight: "In a recent article, a non-Latter-day Saint scholar gave a fresh and most interesting review of this Church and its unpredicted growth since its restoration 160 years ago. He described its growth as a 'miracle' and an 'incredibly rare event.' (Rodney Stark, "The Rise of a New World Faith," *Review of Religious Research,* vol. 26, no. 1, Sept. 1984, 18.)" ("Filling the Whole Earth," *Ensign,* May 1990, 23).

CHAPTER 4

THOSE WHO WARNED US

1. Apparently there were other Nephite survivors, as indicated in Doctrine and Covenants 3:16–19. Elder Bruce R. McConkie said: "There were many Nephite groups, however, who were not destroyed in the final conflict, and these (with possible exceptions) have since mingled themselves with the Lamanites, the resulting peoples being known to the world as the American Indians" (*Mormon Doctrine,* 529).

CHAPTER 5

THE COVENANT ON THE LAND

1. Other references indicate this theme was repeated among the Nephites (1 Nephi 4:14; 13:30; 17:36–38; 2 Nephi 4:4; Enos 1:10; Mosiah 9:3; 11:20–25; 12:2–7; 27:13; 29:18; Alma 9:13, 24; 37:31; 38:1; Helaman 11:37; 13:17, 30; 3 Nephi 1:19; Ether 7:23).

CHAPTER 6

A NATION OF LAW

1. A comparison of the Bible and the Joseph Smith Translation indicates that omissions of basic doctrines are probably more serious than mistranslations (Matthews, *A Bible!* 89–99). Joseph Smith said, "I believe the Bible as it read when it came from the pen of the original writers. Ignorant translators, careless transcribers, or designing and corrupt priests have committed many errors" (*Teachings of the Prophet Joseph Smith,* 327)

2. President Ezra Taft Benson declared in the October 1976 general conference: "We know the signers of the sacred Declaration of Independence and the Founding Fathers, with George Washington at their head, have made appearance in holy places. Apostle Wilford Woodruff was president of the St. George Temple at the time of their appearance and testified that the founders of our republic declared this to him: 'We laid the foundation of the government you now enjoy, and we never apostatized from it, but we remained true to it and were faithful to God.' (*Journal of Discourses,* 19:229.)

"Later, after he became President of the Church, President Woodruff declared that 'those men who laid the foundation of this American government and signed the Declaration of Independence were the best spirits the God of heaven could find on the face of the earth. They were choice spirits, not wicked men. General Washington and all the men who labored for the purpose were inspired of the Lord.' (*Conference Report,* April 1898, p. 89.)" ("Our Priceless Heritage," 34).

3. Most individuals agree that government is essential for certain services—garbage pickup, paved roads, zoning, national defense, etc. But as to the mix of free enterprise and government intervention, even good men have reasonable differences.

4. This difference in political philosophy surfaced in the early days of this republic between the followers of Hamilton and Jefferson, and it is still a current issue between the two major political parties of our day.

5. Prophets have indicated that abortion may be justified only in certain circumstances. Declared President Boyd K. Packer: "Except where the wicked crime of incest or rape was involved, or where competent medical authorities certify

that the life of the mother is in jeopardy, or that a severely defective fetus cannot survive birth, abortion is clearly a 'thou shalt not'" ("Covenants," 85).

CHAPTER 7

FROM RIGHTEOUSNESS TO DESTRUCTION

1. Elder Mark E. Petersen said: "Jacob Wasserman, in his book *Columbus, the Don Quixote of the Seas,* quotes the discoverer as saying: 'The Lord was well disposed to my desire and he bestowed upon me courage and understanding; knowledge of seafaring he gave me in abundance, . . . and of geometry and astronomy—likewise. . . . The Lord with provident hand unlocked my mind, sent me upon the sea, and gave me fire for the deed. Those who heard of my enterprise called it foolish, mocked me, and laughed. But who can doubt that the Holy Ghost inspired me?' (New Brunswick: Rutgers University Press, 1959, pp. 19–20.)

"To King Ferdinand Columbus said: 'I came to your majesty as the emissary of the Holy Ghost,' upon which Wasserman commented:

"'In the same way before that pious assemblage in San Esteban he insisted that he must be regarded as one inspired.' (Page 46.)" (Conference Report, April 1967, 111).

2. The people of Enoch avoided this problem. The record states: "And the Lord called his people Zion, because they were of one heart and one mind, and dwelt in righteousness; and there was no poor among them" (Moses 7:18).

3. Only repentance can save them at this point (Helaman 5:17; 5:50–52; 11:11–15, 17; 11:34; 12:23–24; 13:8, 10; 15:1–3, 7, 17; 3 Nephi 3:15; 4:29–30, 33; 3 Nephi 8:24–25; 9:13–14; 10:4–6).

4. See also Helaman 8:26; 11:36–37; 13:12–14; 16:12, 15; 3 Nephi 6:18; Ether 2:9. See also the Doctrine and Covenants 18:6; 61:31.

5. Apparently some Nephites survived, as indicated in Doctrine and Covenants 3:16–19. Elder Bruce R. McConkie said: "There were many Nephite groups, however, who were not destroyed in the final conflict, and these (with possible exceptions) have since mingled themselves with the Lamanites, the resulting peoples being known to the world as the *American Indians*" (*Mormon Doctrine,* 529).

6. See, for example, the warning voices in Helaman 10:11, 14; 13:5–10, 30, 32, 38; 3 Nephi 2:13, 19.

7. See Helaman 3:3, 17; 4:1; 10:18, 11:22; 3 Nephi 2:11. For the curse upon the land and final destruction, see 3 Nephi 3:24; 6:18; 7:14; 8:12–22; 9:2–12. Only the righteous survived the destruction that preceded the appearance of the Savior in the Americas. Mormon and Moroni saw the entire destruction of

their people (Mormon 4–6) and preserved the record of the destruction of the Jaredites (Ether 15:29–32).

CHAPTER 8
THE FALL OF THE ANTEDILUVIANS

1. LDS Bible Dictionary, s.v. "Bible Chronology," 635–36. The term *antediluvian* means "of the period before the biblical flood."

2. On the birth of Adam, see Matthews, *A Bible!* 168–95, especially 188.

3. President Ezra Taft Benson declared: "America is a place of many great events. Here is where Adam dwelt, where the Garden of Eden was located. America was the place of former civilizations, including Adam's, the Jaredites,' and Nephites.' America is also the place where God the Father and His Son, Jesus Christ, appeared to Joseph Smith, inaugurating the last gospel dispensation on earth before the Savior's second coming" ("Witness and a Warning," 31).

4. In the premortal life, we were brothers and sisters to each other, sons and daughters unto God, but not until this probationary state were we given the opportunity to become husband and wife, father and mother. Marriage and procreation would not have been available to us had we remained forever as spirits.

5. The plan of salvation, like the plan mortal parents have for their children, calls for the children to move away from their parents' home when they are sufficiently mature and prepared. Children must find out for themselves, away from the immediate presence of their parents, if what their parents taught them is true, efficacious, and practical.

6. Doctrine and Covenants 133:24: "And the land of Jerusalem and the land of Zion shall be turned back into their own place, and the earth shall be like as it was in the days before it was divided."

CHAPTER 10
THE RISE AND FALL OF THE NEPHITES AND MULEKITES

1. When Martin Harris lost the 116 manuscript pages, the Lord instructed Joseph Smith not to begin again at the place where the first 116 pages originated— Mormon's abridgment of the large plates. Consequently, our present Book of Mormon begins with the small plates of Nephi and his personal account of his family leaving Jerusalem.

2. See Mosiah 1:78; 2:22, 31; 9:9; 10:5, 15; 23:19; 25:24; 29:32; Alma 9:13, 16; 36:1; 38:1; 45:8, 16; 46:17; 48:15, 25; 50:20; 3 Nephi 20:14, 29; 21:22.

3. See 1 Nephi 17:35; 2 Nephi 28:16; Mosiah 12:12; Alma 10:19; 26:5; 37:28, 31; 45:16; Helaman 5:2; 6:40; 8:26; 11:36–37; 16:12, 15; 3 Nephi 6:18, and Ether 2:15.

CHAPTER 11

THE SURVIVAL OF THE LAMANITES

1. Later in the Book of Mormon record, those who followed the Lamanites, regardless of their ethnic origin, were called Lamanites (Jacob 1:14; 4 Nephi 1:37–38).

2. The curse of Laman and Lemuel was to be cut off from revelation, from an inspired father and prophet-brother (2 Nephi 5:20, 24–25; Alma 23:18). The Lamanites had prophets for a short time, most notably Samuel, a prophet to both Nephites and Lamanites, but he is mentioned only briefly in the record. The skin pigmentation was a mark or sign to prevent intermarriage between the Nephites and the Lamanites, but it was not the curse itself (2 Nephi 5:21–23).

CHAPTER 12

THE FATE OF THE GENTILES

1. Many churches have come from a variety of biblical interpretations. The Holy Ghost, as a gift, can only be given by the priesthood authority restored by Peter, James, and John, to the Prophet Joseph Smith and Oliver Cowdery.

2. In November 2003, for example, the Supreme Court of Massachusetts declared that same-gender marriage is on par with heterosexual marriage. The court mandated that by May 2004 same-gender marriages in that state were to be given the same benefits and legal status as a traditional marriage.

3. President Spender W. Kimball stated: "We realize that while all men definitely should, all men are not prepared to teach the gospel abroad. Far too many young men arrive at the missionary age quite unprepared to go on a mission, and of course *they should not be sent*. But they should all be prepared" ("When the World Will Be Converted," 8; italics added).

4. McConkie, "Coming Tests and Trials and Glory," 73.

5. Though historians credit various factors, including the tension between the industrial states and the agricultural states, or slavery, or a number of things, as primary determinants of the Civil War, the principle of casting out the righteous also comes into play as indicated in this revelation to President Brigham Young (see also D&C 45:63; 89:6, 7; 130:12, 13).

CHAPTER 13

THE ROLE OF THE LATTER-DAY SAINTS

1. In April 2004 a delegation from Illinois traveled to Utah with a formal apology for the way the Saints were treated in being cast out of the state more than a century and half before.

Sources

Andersen, H. Verlan. "Missionary Work Is the Lifeblood of the Church." *Ensign,* November 1986, 23–24.

Ballard, M. Russell. "His Word Ye Shall Receive." *Ensign,* May 2001, 65–67.

———. "The Joy of Hope Fulfilled." *Ensign,* November 1992, 31–33.

———. "The Kingdom Rolls Forth in South America." *Ensign,* May 1986, 12–15.

Benson, Ezra Taft. "The Book of Mormon Is the Word of God." *Ensign,* May 1975, 63–65.

———. "The Book of Mormon—Keystone of Our Religion." *Ensign,* November 1986, 4–7.

———. "Flooding the Earth with the Book of Mormon." *Ensign,* November 1988, 4–6.

———. "A Message to the World." *Ensign,* November 1975, 32–34.

———. "Our Divine Constitution," *Ensign,* November 1987, 4–7.

———. "Our Priceless Heritage." *Ensign,* November 1976, 33–35.

———. *The Teachings of Ezra Taft Benson.* Salt Lake City: Bookcraft, 1988.

———. "A Witness and a Warning." *Ensign,* November 1979, 31–33.

Clark, James R., ed. *Message of the First Presidency of The Church of Jesus Christ of Latter-day Saints.* 6 vols. Salt Lake City: Bookcraft, 1965–75.

Haight, David B. "A Call to Serve." *Ensign,* November 1988, 82–85.

Hinckley, Gordon B. "At the Summit of the Ages." *Ensign,* November 1999, 72–74.

———. "The Dawning of a Brighter Day." *Ensign,* May 2004, 81–84.

———. "An Ensign to the Nations, a Light to the World." *Ensign,* November 2003, 82–85.

———. "Look to the Future." *Ensign,* November 1997, 67–69.

———. *Teachings of Gordon B. Hinckley.* Salt Lake City: Deseret Book, 1997.

———. "The Times in Which We Live." *Ensign,* November 2001, 72–74.

———. "Walking in the Light of the Lord." *Ensign,* November 1998, 97–100.

———. "We Need Not Fear His Coming." *Speeches of the Year, 1979.* Provo, Utah: Brigham Young University Press, 1980.

Hunter, Howard W. *Teachings of Howard W. Hunter.* Edited by Clyde J. Williams. Salt Lake City: Bookcraft, 1996.

Journal of Discourses. 26 vols. London: Latter-day Saints' Book Depot, 1854–86.

Kimball, Spencer W. "Listen to the Prophet's Voice." *Improvement Era,* December 1961, 936–41.

———. "The False Gods We Worship." *Ensign,* June 1976, 3–6.

———. "Families Can Be Eternal." *Ensign,* November 1980, 4–5.

———. "The Stone Cut without Hands." *Ensign,* May 1976, 4–9.

———. "When the World Will Be Converted." *Ensign,* October 1974, 2–14.

Lee, Harold B. *The Teachings of Harold B. Lee.* Edited by Clyde J. Williams. Salt Lake City: Bookcraft, 1997.

———. *Ye Are the Light of the World.* Salt Lake City: Deseret Book, 1974.

Matthews, Robert J. *A Bible! A Bible!* Salt Lake City: Bookcraft, 1990.

Maxwell, Neal A. "The Great Plan of the Eternal God." *Ensign,* May 1984, 21–23.

McConkie, Bruce R. "Come: Let Israel Build Zion." *Ensign,* May 1977, 115–18.

———. "The Coming Tests and Trials and Glory." *Ensign,* May 1980, 71–73.

———. *Mormon Doctrine.* 2d ed. Salt Lake City: Bookcraft, 1966.

"News of the Church: First Presidency Warns Against 'Irreligion.'" *Ensign,* May 1979, 108–9.

Oaks, Dallin H. "The Great Plan of Happiness." *Ensign,* November 1993, 72–75.

Packer, Boyd K. "Covenants." *Ensign,* November 1990, 84–86.

———. "The Father and the Family." *Ensign,* May 1994, 19–21.

———. "The One Pure Defense." Address to Church Educational System religious educators, Salt Lake City, Utah, 6 February 2004.

———. "Our Moral Environment." *Ensign,* May 1992, 66–68.

Petersen, Mark E. Conference Report, April 1967, 111–14.

———. *Noah and the Flood.* Salt Lake City: Deseret Book, 1982.

SOURCES

Smith, Joseph. *History of The Church of Jesus Christ of Latter-day Saints.* Edited by B. H. Roberts. 2d ed. rev. 7 vols. Salt Lake City: The Church of Jesus Christ of Latter-day Saints, 1932–51.

———. *Teachings of the Prophet Joseph Smith.* Selected by Joseph Fielding Smith. Salt Lake City: Deseret Book, 1976.

Smith, Joseph F. Conference Report. April 1880, 95–96.

The World Almanac and Book of Facts. Edited by Mark S. Hoffman. New York: Pharos Books, 1993.

Index